Old Chryston and Muirhead

by John Hood

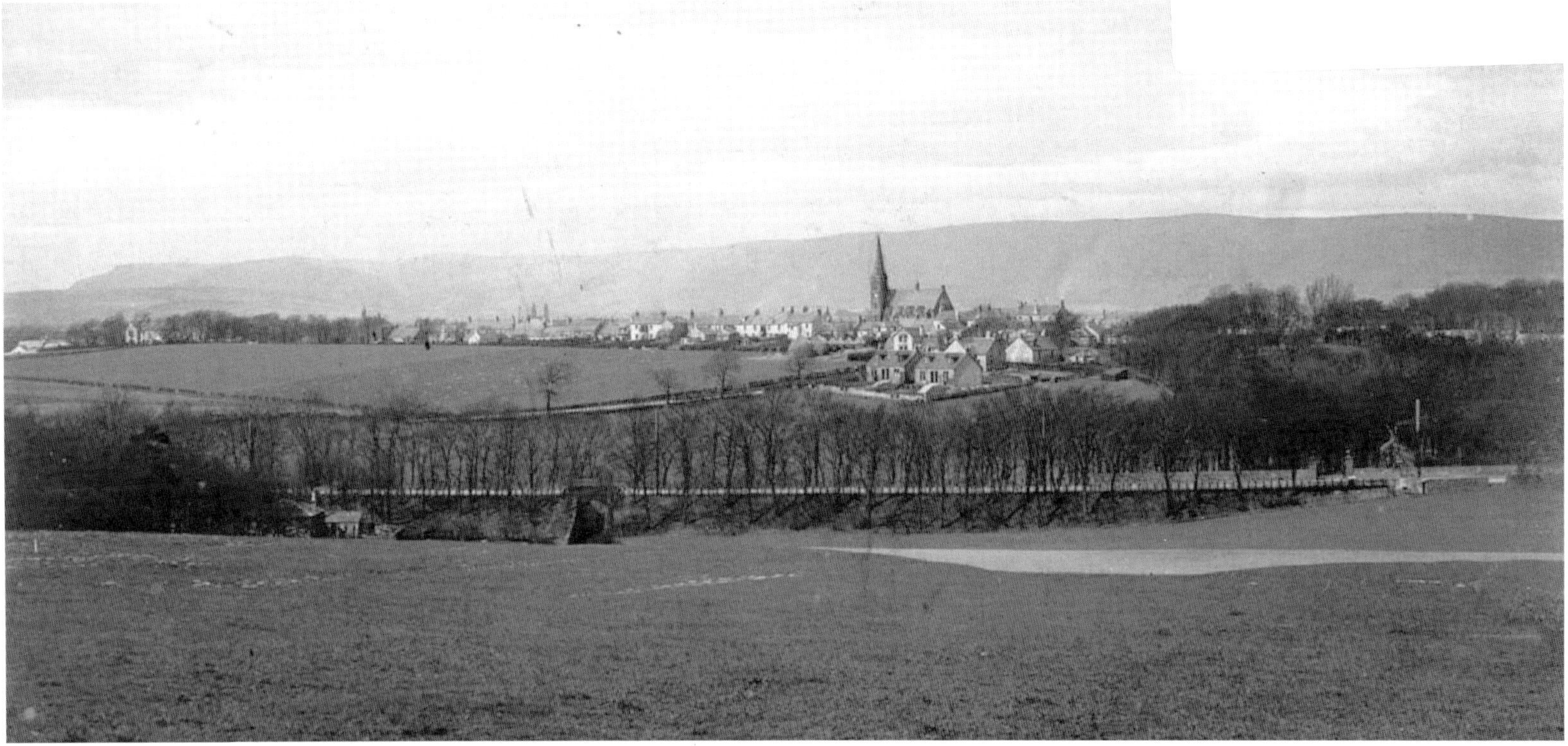

With its 110-foot high spire, Chryston Parish Church on Main Street (seen here in 1908) is the most prominent landmark in the village – indeed the spire is visible for miles around. Incorporated into the spire is a four-faced clock, which was installed in 1884. This clock was actually added to the spire some six years after the church was built, when the new laird, Colonel Sir Alexander Sprot of Garnkirk (on his first visit to the district), happened to remark to the then minister 'how much better' the church would be if the spire had a clock. This suggestion was promptly taken up, and in due course the necessary funds were raised by subscriptions received from Sir Alexander (who subsequently unveiled the clock) and other prominent local people. Also seen to the mid-left of the picture (and to the left of Chryston Road), are fields belonging to Chryston Mains Farm – note the haystacks in the corner of the field. In the 1920s these fields were taken for council housing, although those on the south side of Cumbernauld Road (seen here in the foreground) have remained undeveloped.

First published in the United Kingdom, 2009,
by Stenlake Publishing Ltd.
www.stenlake.co.uk
ISBN 9781840334760

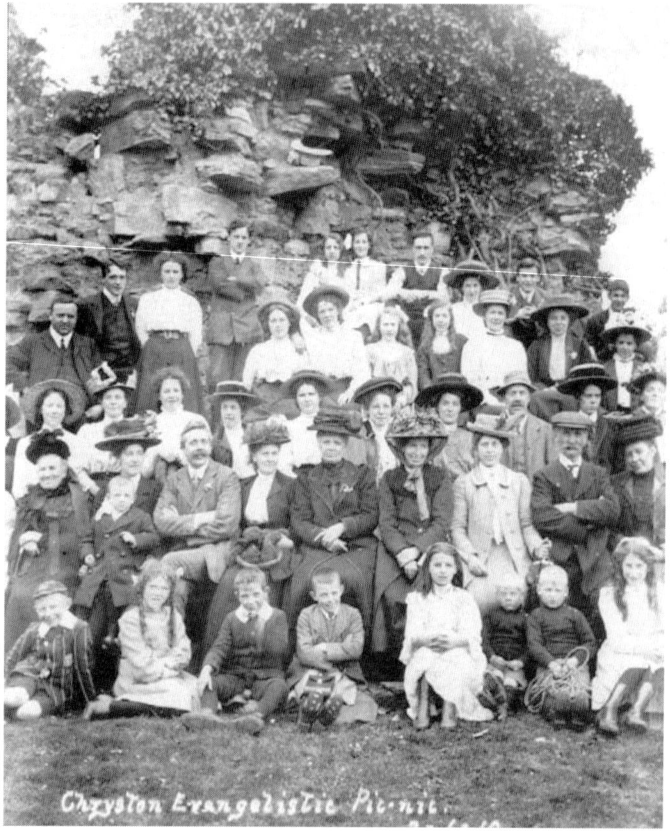

On Thursday, 2 June 1910 (coincidently also Victoria Day) members of several of the local churches left Chryston for their annual picnic. Invariably, the starting point for such picnics was Garnkirk Station, and thence by train to destinations as varied as Inversnaid, Killin and Luss. Because of the large numbers involved, special trains were often laid on. This particular photograph is of Muirhead Evangelistic Hall Bible Class and, on this occasion in 1910, they were heading for Tullietudlem, near Lanark. As befitted the occasion, most of the ladies were wearing their bonnets, some of them very fancy! As was the custom, the picnickers, on reaching their destination, were provided with eats. Often these were prepared locally and, together with tea urns and kettles, were then conveyed in large wicker hampers to the chosen picnic site. In 1901, for example, it is recorded that the parish church picnic required '600 bags of bread and sixty gallons of milk'! An alteration to this tradition occurred during times of war, when, because of rationing, picnickers were sometimes asked to bring their own food.

Acknowledgments

I would like to thank the following for their help: Muriel Backhouse, Rubina Baxter, James Bryant, Alexandra Cannon, Mrs Francis Clark, Steve Cook, Iain Findlay, Jim Findlay, Miss Florence Haining, Theresa Hinds, Jacqueline Hone, Mhoira and George Jamieson, Janet Irvine, John Keith, Ena McKay, Allan McKenzie (Local Studies Librarian, North Lanarkshire Council), Roger McLean, Bill Moodie, Anne Peters, Nancy Stewart, Irene Stirling, Moira Tait, Grace Trotter, Johnston Wilkieson, and Oswald and Irene Wright. Last, but by no means least, I should like to thank Don Martin, Reference & Information Librarian, East Dunbartonshire Council, for reading through and commenting on the manuscript, although, ultimately, of course, the responsibility for any errors or omissions remains mine. The publishers wish to thank East Dumbartonshire Council for permission to reproduce the photographs on pages 27, 37, 38, 41, 46, 47, 49, 50, 54 and 55

Further Reading

The books listed below were used by the author during his research. None of them are available from Stenlake Publishing. Those interested in finding out more are advised to contact their local bookshop or local studies library.

Duthie, William S., *Chryston: A North Lanarkshire Village*, Strathkelvin District Libraries, 1987.

Kidd, Neil, *The Story of Chryston*, Strathkelvin District Libraries, 1993.

Martin, Don, *The Garnkirk & Glasgow Railway*, Strathkelvin District Libraries, 1981.

Strathkelvin Mining Project Team, *Bridgend: A Scottish Colliery Village*, Strathkelvin District Libraries, 1984.

Introduction

Until 1930, when they were transferred into the newly formed Lower Ward of Lanark County Council, the adjoining villages of Chryston, Moodiesburn and Muirhead had been located within Cadder Parish. The first (and oldest) of these villages was Chryston, or 'Christ's Town' as it was earlier known. Originally it formed part of the old estate of Bedlay and the Mollins, which had been given to the Bishopric of Glasgow by King William the Lion in the twelfth century, but which later passed into the hands of the Earls of Kilmarnock. Until the 1780s, when a new turnpike road was formed half a mile to the south of Chryston, the village had to some extent prospered due to its position on the old Glasgow–Stirling highway; however, as late as 1831, its population still numbered less than 400. The village, which was then described as having 'remarkable cleanliness of aspect', largely consisted of one-storey thatched cottages which lined both sides of Main Street. These cottages, some of which remain today, were inhabited mainly by weavers and agricultural workers. Within thirty years the population had increased to 617, and the village could then boast of having two churches (each with large manses), three schools and the inevitably well-patronised public house. Although by then a thriving little community, its reliance on local wells for water (for both drinking and washing) hampered its further development. This problem was finally solved in the mid 1880s, when mains carrying water (piped from Glasgow Corporation's waterworks at Loch Katrine) were laid down. Shortly afterwards, in 1910, the villagers' lives were further enhanced when gas mains were laid to bring in gas (again courtesy of Glasgow Corporation), to replace the paraffin lamps previously used for domestic and street lighting. Within eighteen years, the gas lamps were themselves replaced by electricity supplied by the Clyde Valley Electrical Power Company. The period between 1860 and 1900 saw a dramatic increase in the population of the village to around 4,400. This, however, was not brought about by the introduction of the above-mentioned utilities, but by the opening of large fireclay works in the vicinity of Cardowan, Garnkirk and Heathfield. These works, together with an expansion of the railway network, provided further impetus to the development of Chryston – and, to an even greater extent, the neighbouring village of Muirhead.

Despite its advantageous location on the turnpike road, which ran through its main street, and the siting of a toll house there, Muirhead (whose name literally translates as 'the head of the muir') only had a population of less than fifty by 1831. However, this situation changed dramatically when there became a need for accommodation for fireclay workers and, later, miners. The 1831 opening of a station at Garnkirk, on the Garnkirk & Glasgow (Gartsherrie–Glasgow) railway line, also eventually lead to an increase in population. As a consequence, more facilities were required and by the late nineteenth century the village had an inn, a public hall (shared with Chryston), an evangelistic hall, a masonic lodge, a police station, a post office, and a new public school. There was also an increase in the number of shops and these offered a wide range of goods and services. Although rail travel did decline from the 1920s onwards, this was more than compensated by the number of bus companies operating in the district.

The nearby hamlet of Moodiesburn first gained prominence due to its position on the new turnpike road to the east of Muirhead. In 1805, because it was located on a recognised stagecoach route between Glasgow, Stirling and Edinburgh, coaches operated by the New North Star Company regularly stopped at the Old Inn in Moodiesburn. From 1900 onwards, however, all further expansion took place to the north of the hamlet, influenced by the opening of a colliery at Auchengeich. This latter development not only gave rise to an increase in the local population, but also created the mining village of Bridgend which was built by coal masters James Nimmo & Company at the turn of the twentieth century to provide accommodation for the colliery miners and their families. While the later decline of the local fireclay industry had a negative effect on the population of the district as a whole, the subsequent closure of the colliery following a disastrous fire in 1959 had a dramatic effect on Bridgend. This village, which in 1923 was described as an 'up-to-date modern colliery village', comprised rows of single- and two-storey houses. These houses, approximately 104 in number, were of the room-and-kitchen type and had inside toilets and sculleries, as well as shared wash houses and ash pits. A welfare hall was opened in 1923, followed five years later by an outdoor bowling green and tennis courts. However, the inevitable exodus of the miners and their families from the area following closure of the pit meant that, by the mid 1960s, the village was virtually deserted, and now no longer exists.

This decrease in local population was to some extent compensated for by the large number of council houses being built on the Gartferry Estate to the north of Moodiesburn from the 1930s until the 1970s. This, together with similar council housing schemes in Chryston and Muirhead, resulted in an increase in the local population, and inevitably new churches and schools had to be built to serve it. In the last thirty to forty years, despite the loss of the colliery and the last of the local fireclay works shutting down in the early 1960s, the area has also benefited from its proximity to the industrial and commercial centres of Glasgow and Edinburgh, which have been brought ever closer by successive improvements to the A80 dual carriageway. This has resulted in a significant increase in private housing, particularly in Moodiesburn, where the erection of private housing estates by several major house builders has meant that it now has a larger population than that of Chryston and Muirhead combined. Today, the majority of the population of these villages now work outwith the local area.

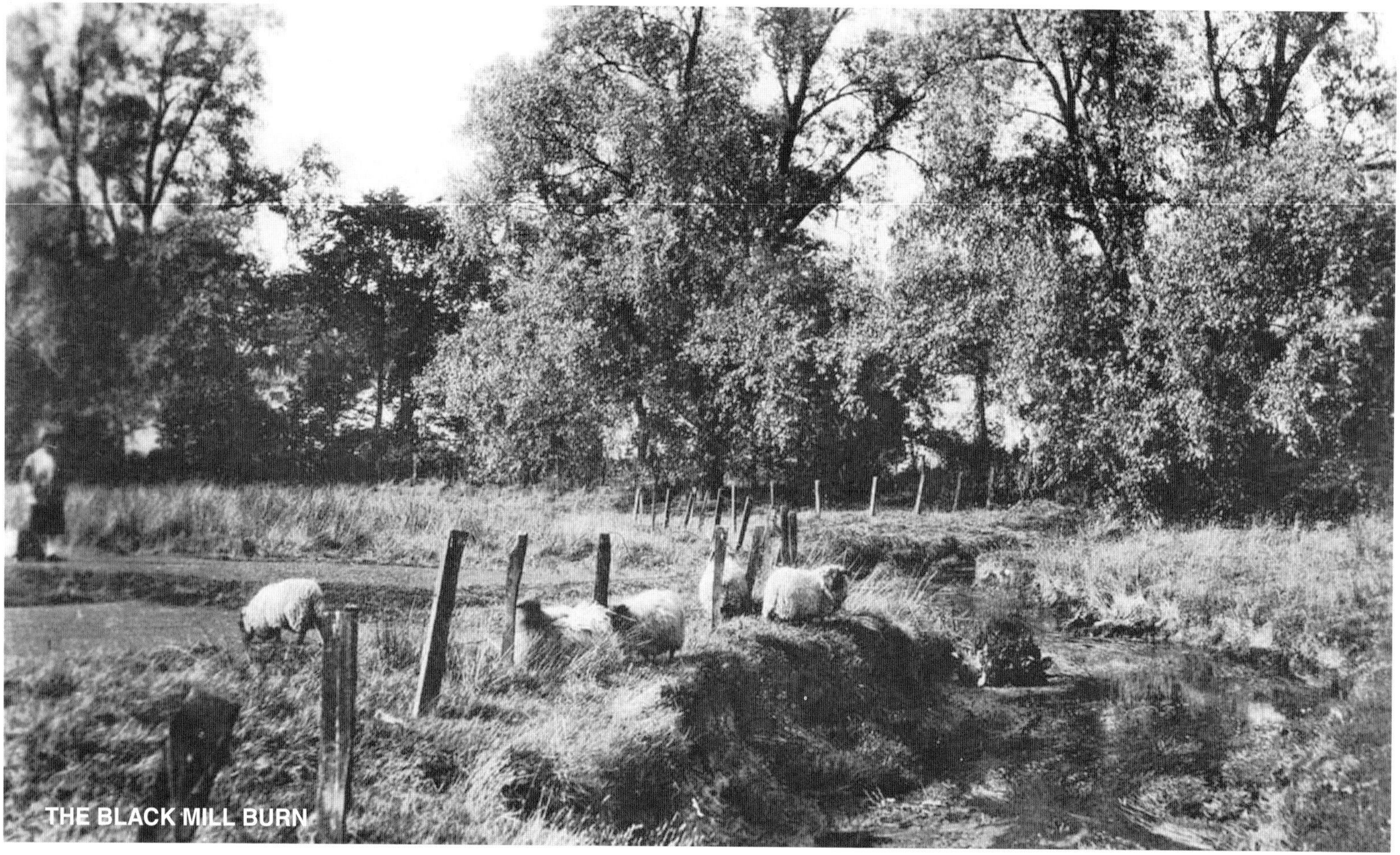

The Black Mill Burn is most probably a stretch of the Bothlyn Burn, or of one of its tributaries. The reference to 'mill' may come from the old Mill of Bedlay, which was used for grinding corn. This mill and miller's house (which were demolished around the 1840s) were located on the Bothlyn Burn just below Bedlay House, in the field known locally as the 'mill field'. On the other hand, the burn pictured here may be the Black Burn. In 1898, this burn was recorded as being rendered undrinkable for cattle due to coal washing at nearby Meiklehill; as a result, in times of drought, farmers had to cart water from a gravitational supply at the colliery. This problem of pollution of the local burns was a constant one over the years and led to the Kirkintilloch Farmers' Union complaining generally about pollution in 1917.

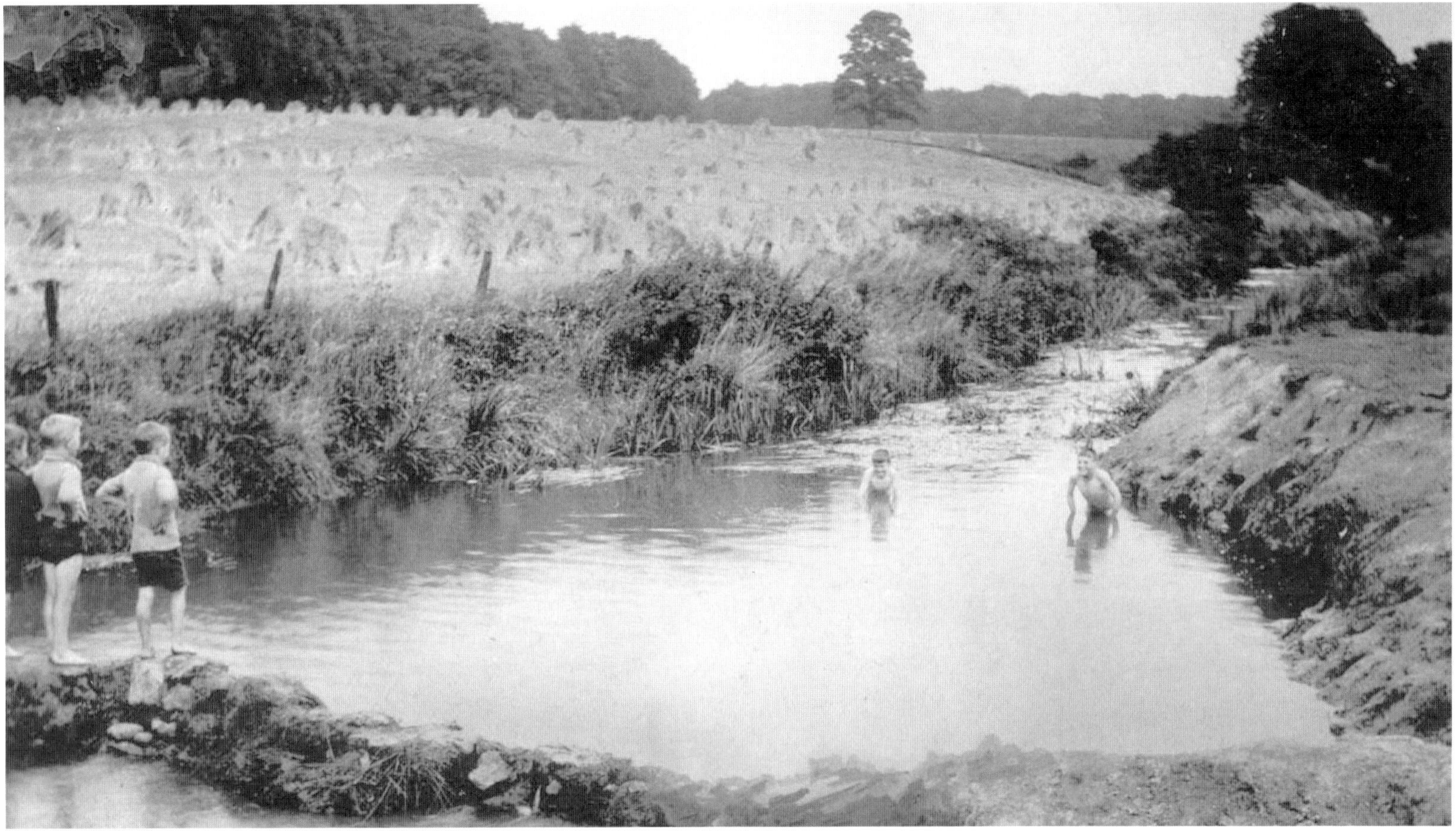

This particular stretch of the Bothlyn Burn, known locally as Wilkie's Burn, took its name from William Wilkie, the then occupant of nearby Gartferry House. Although it may at one time have been perfectly safe to drink water from the Bothlyn Burn, from the late 1800s onwards, large stretches of the burn were frequently polluted by domestic and industrial waste. Notwithstanding, the burn was well used by local children, who fished there for burn trout and 'baggie minnows'. As this 1930s photograph shows, it was also used to swim in, having been efficiently dammed with stones and clods of earth to form a rudimentary swimming pool! Although most of the pollution entered the burn further downstream, these swimmers would still have been in danger of ending up with 'orange' legs, due to the waste that was discharged into the burn from Smith & McLean's Steel and Iron Works in Gartcosh. Further downstream at Bridgend the burn was also used, prior to the opening of pithead baths at Auchengeich Colliery in 1931, for bathing by the miners and their families, as their homes were not then equipped with bathrooms.

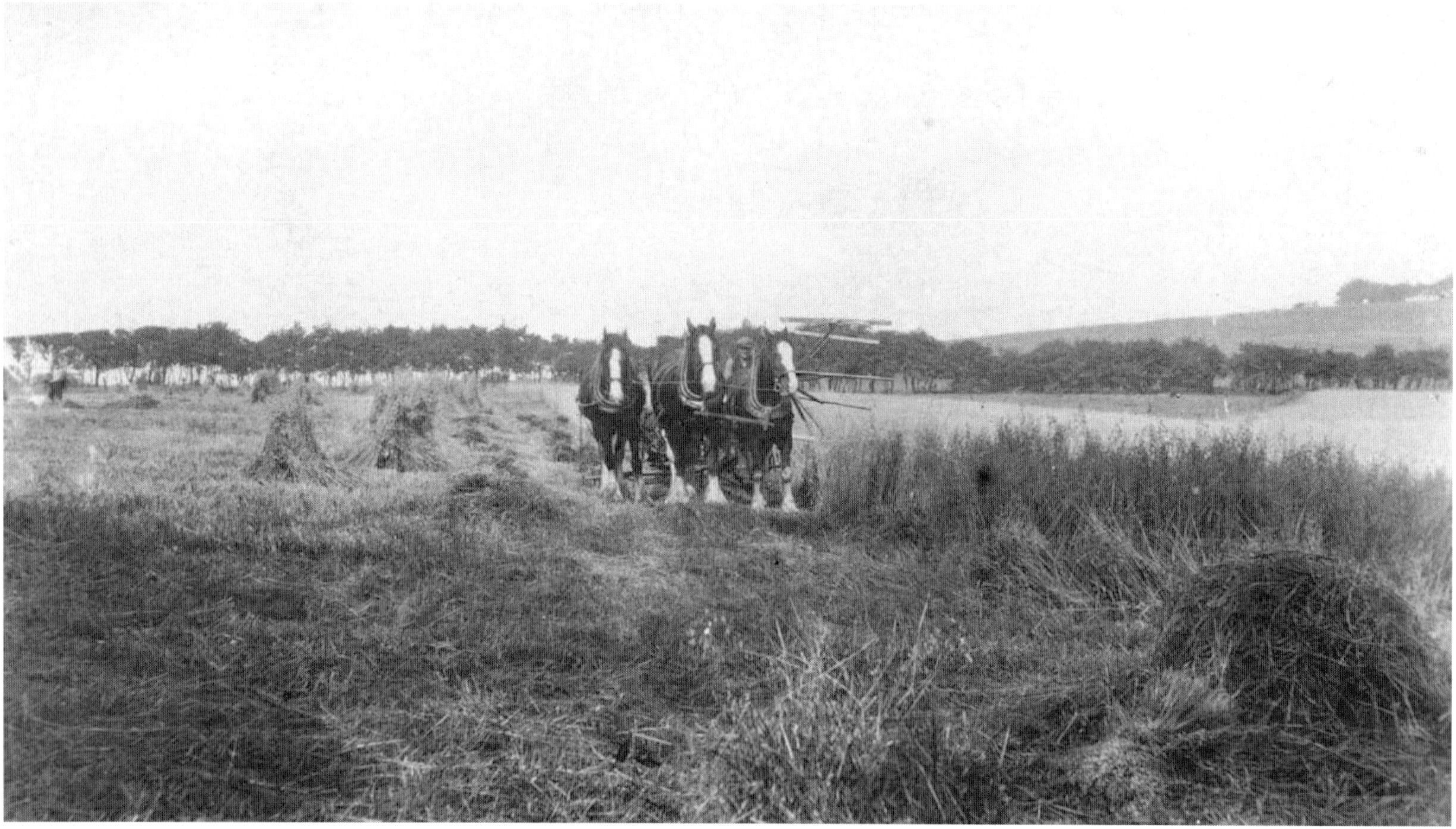

In the 1930s, when this photograph was taken at Holms Farm, Muirhead, much of the heavy work around farms was still undertaken by teams of Clydesdale horses. The very best of these horses – such as the legendary Baron of Buchlyvie, which was sold in 1911 for £9,500 – were retained for breeding purposes. The most prominent of the local breeders was Robert Chapman, who farmed at Johnston Farm, Gartcosh. Chapman, who died in 1913, bred several outstanding champion Clydesdales, including the engagingly named Winsome Baroness. This interest in Clydesdales was continued by Robert Chapman's youngest son, James, who, in addition to being an Honorary President of the Clydesdale Horse Society, won the Cawder Cup for the champion Clydesdale of the year on no less than six separate occasions between 1961 and 1970. Another son, Robert, was a noted dog breeder whose Scottie, Heather Realisation, was reported on its death in 1937 to be the 'most famous in the show world'. Although by 1911 there were said to be an estimated 140,000 working Clydesdales in Scotland, the need for greater efficiency during the Second World War saw many of these horses being replaced by tractors.

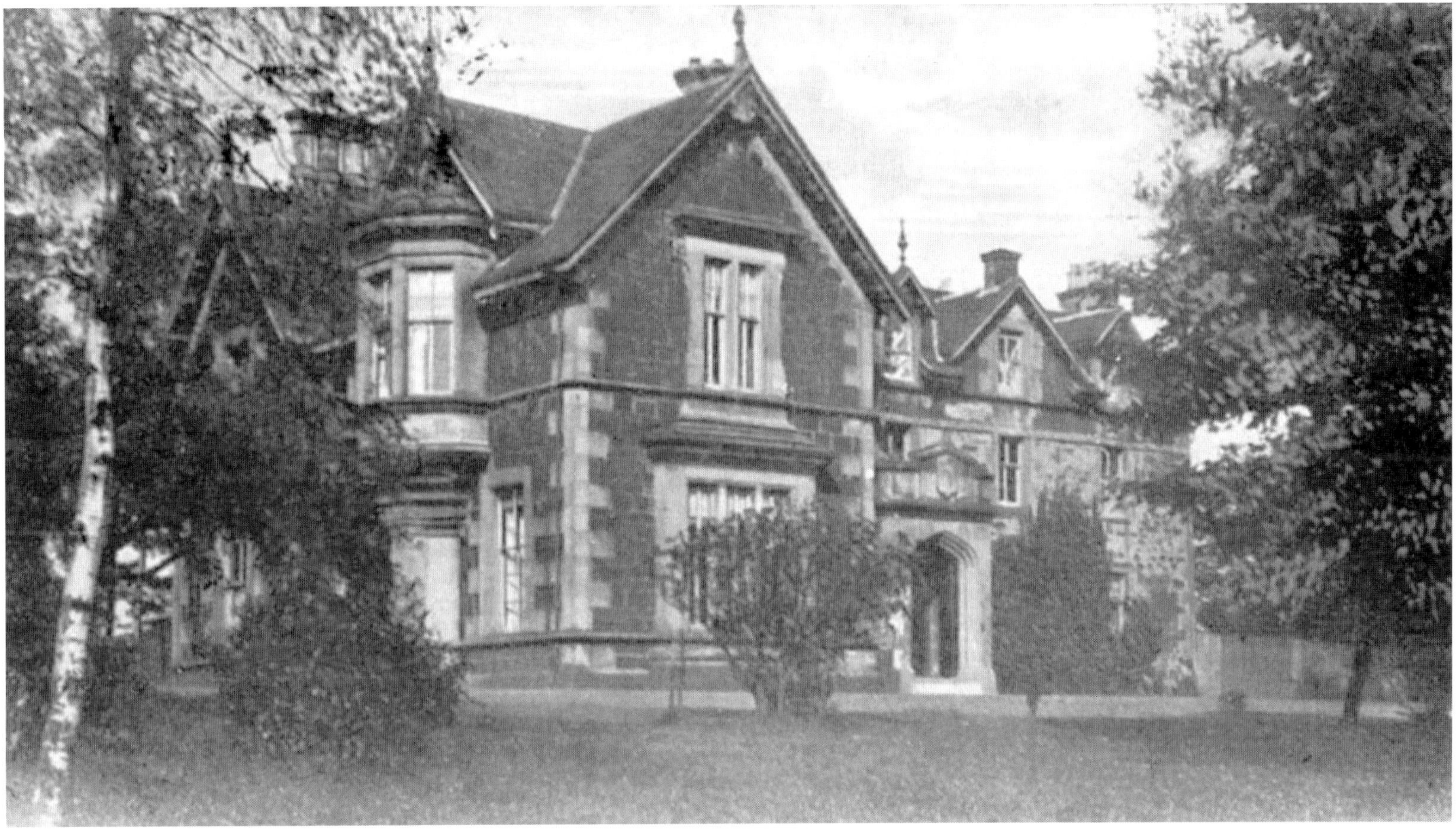

Glaudhall House – the frontage of which is seen here in this 1904 photograph – stands on high ground overlooking Muirhead. Externally at least, it is largely unchanged today. The earlier portion of the house (which is out of view) dates from around 1750, while the newer portion (seen here) dates from the 1850s. Among the house's occupants have been Alexander A. Keith, Chairman of the Cadder Area School Management Committee, who lived in the house from about 1912 until 1940. During the Second World War, the house provided shelter for squatters. In 1947, the house, together with adjacent coach house and stables, was bought by Gartcosh man, Thomas Wilkieson. Thomas had left school at thirteen to go down the mines, before later training to be a motor mechanic with local haulage contractors, Hugh Clelland & Sons. Despite having no previous farming experience, Thomas successfully converted the estate into a farm, retaining the house as a farmhouse, and converting the coach house and stables into a piggery and a barn for beef cows respectively. The farm was later further developed by his son, John.

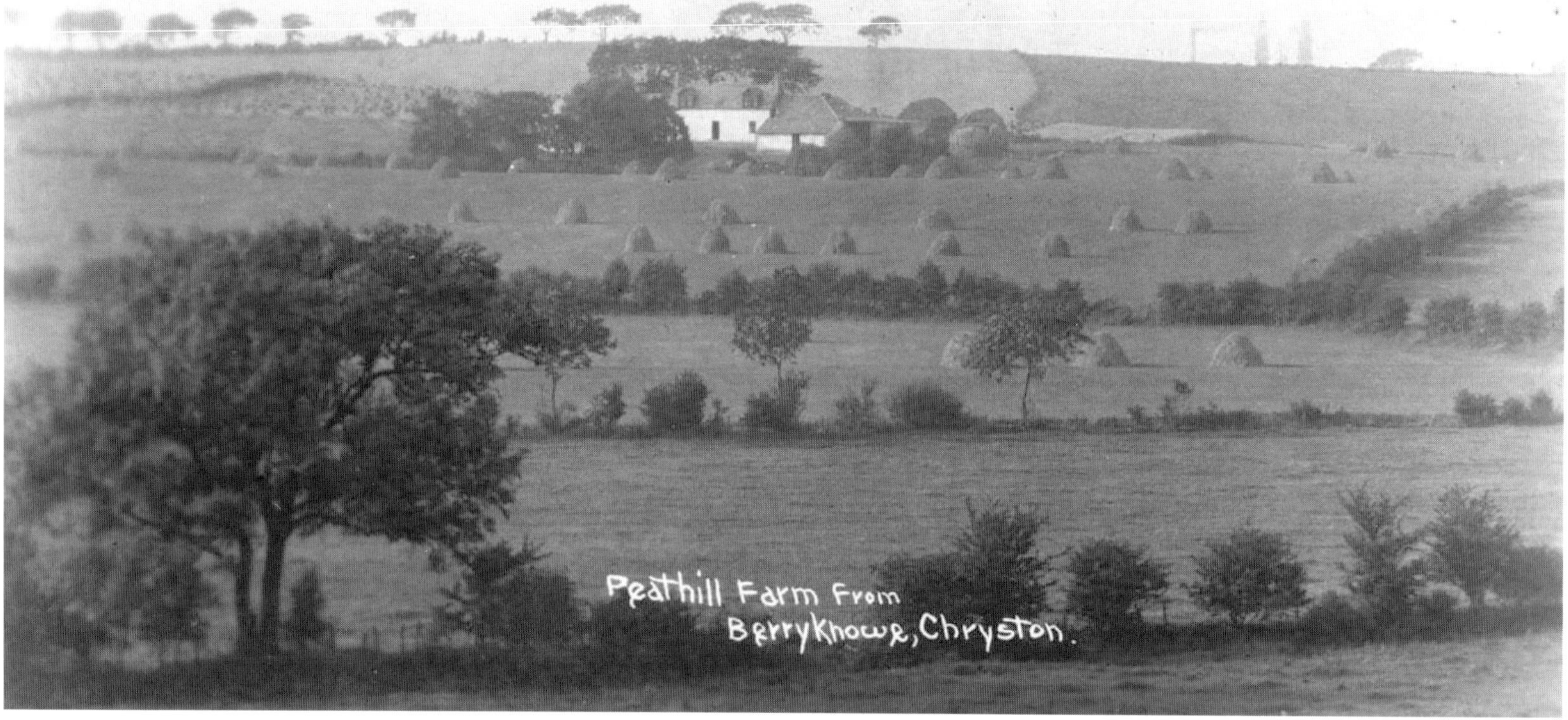

In this early view of Peathill Farm, taken from Berryknowe Farm, the surrounding fields are dotted with haystacks. Located alongside Lindsaybeg Road, Peathill is one of the older farms in the Muirhead area. In 1893 it was farmed by John Shaw, and in the early 1900s was in the hands of the Jackson family. In common with other farms on the nearby Garnkirk Estate, it was put up for sale in 1925 by Colonel Sir Alexander Sprot. Identified in the sale catalogue as Lot No. 23, it then comprised a farmhouse and assorted farm buildings. In the 1940s the farm was owned by the Wilkinson family and then, later, by Robert Cameron, who was the last person to farm there. In 1978, having lain empty for a few years, it was sold to its present owner, who demolished the farmhouse and the attached milk house and built a new house on its site. The house at Berryknowe Farm (which was also at one time owned by the Jackson family) was destroyed by fire in October 1928 and later rebuilt.

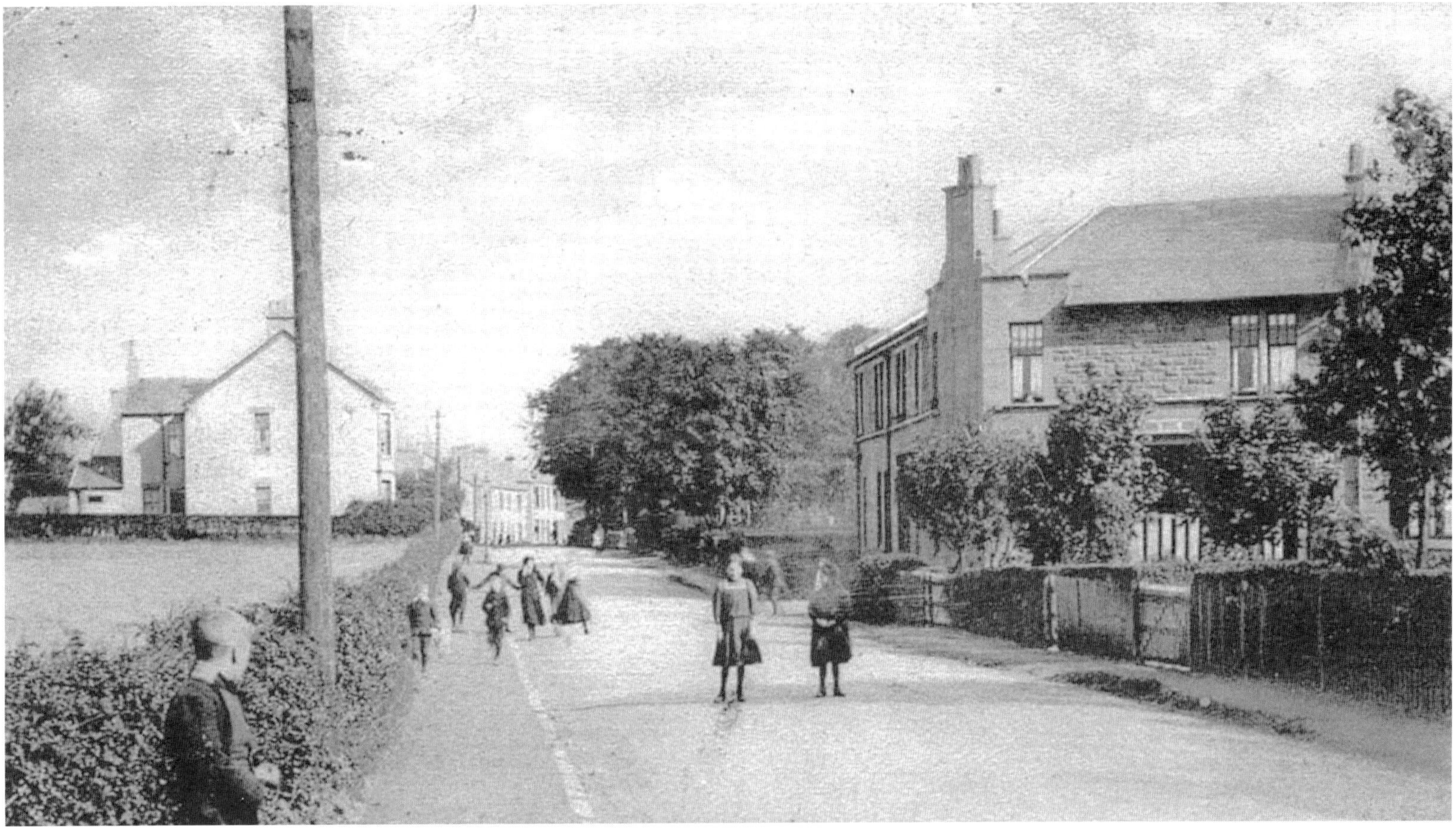

In this photograph of Main Street, Chryston, taken looking east around 1914, the large red sandstone property on the right was known locally as Chapman's Building. It was built around the time of the First World War for Robert Chapman, whose business interests at the time of his death in 1913 included several licensed premises within Cadder Parish. Although it had been Robert's intention to also incorporate a public house within this property, he was unable to secure a licence so instead turned the building into houses of the 'room-and-kitchen' type. In the mid 1920s, the property was sold to the owners of the nearby Auchengeich Colliery and renamed Auchengeich Terrace. In 1948, when the coal industry was nationalised, it became the property of the National Coal Board (NCB). It was given a facelift by the NCB in 1956, but was ultimately demolished in the early 1980s and the Solway Place houses for senior citizens built on its site. Beyond, but largely hidden by the trees, is the entrance to the parish church manse and, opposite, the western gable of the tenement which sits alongside the West End Cottages.

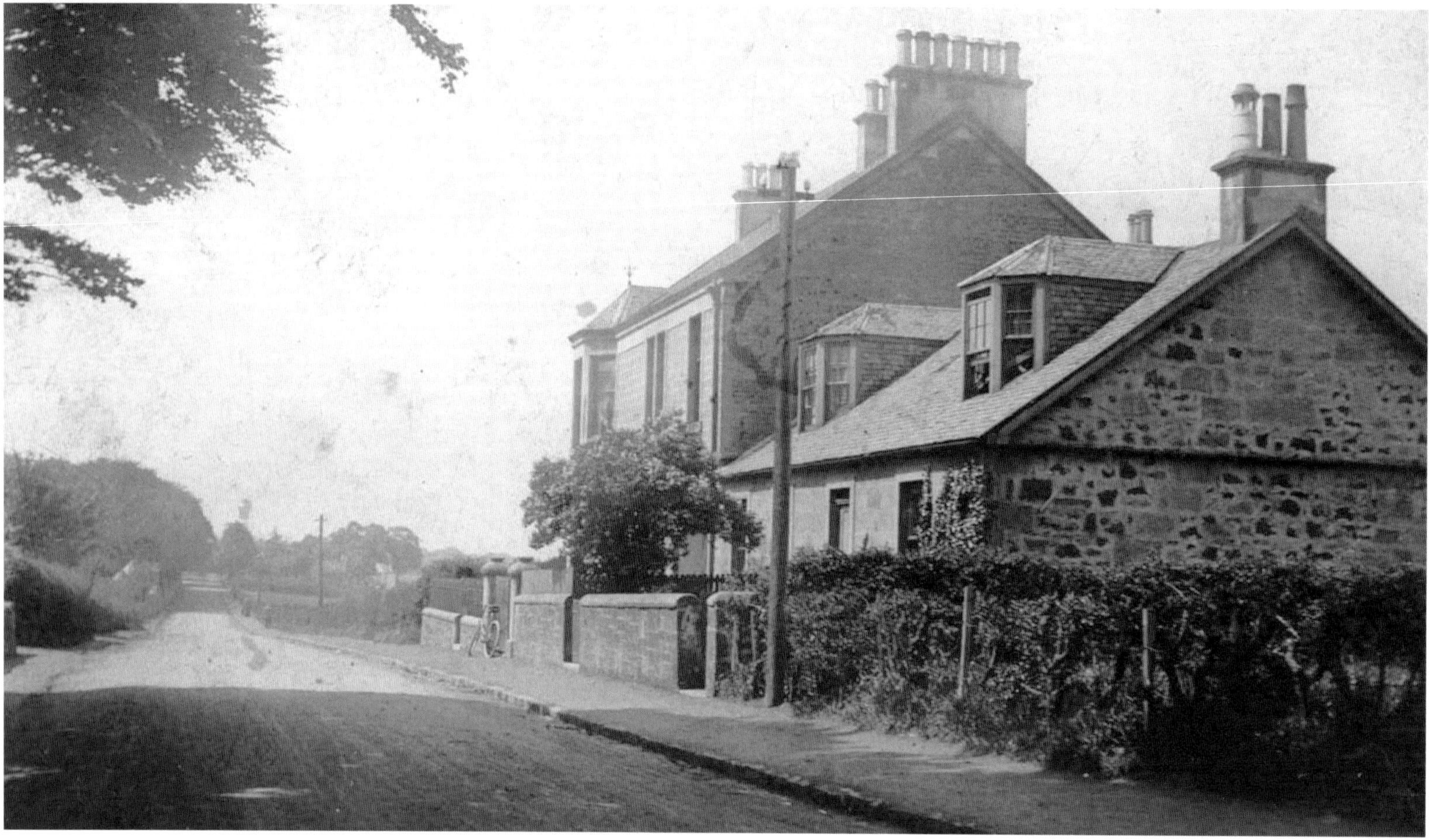

Chryston Main Street, photographed around 1910, with the West End Cottages and an attached two-storey grey sandstone tenement on the right. The latter, which incorporates a pend giving access to the rear of the property, was built by the well-respected local building contractor Robert Mitchell, who ran his business from here. In 1910, shortly before his death, he sold the business to another local building contractor, Allan Bros., Watson & Henderson. In his obituary, it was said of Mitchell that his 'handicraft work is well scattered over the district, having built the greater part of Muirhead and Stepps villadom'. On the opposite side of the street, the low stone wall marks the entrance to Prospect Cottage. Also known locally as McCall's Building, this cottage was at one time the residence of John McCall, who was one of several local carriage hirers that had, prior to the introduction of local omnibus services, provided a much-needed service between Chryston and the railway station at Garnkirk.

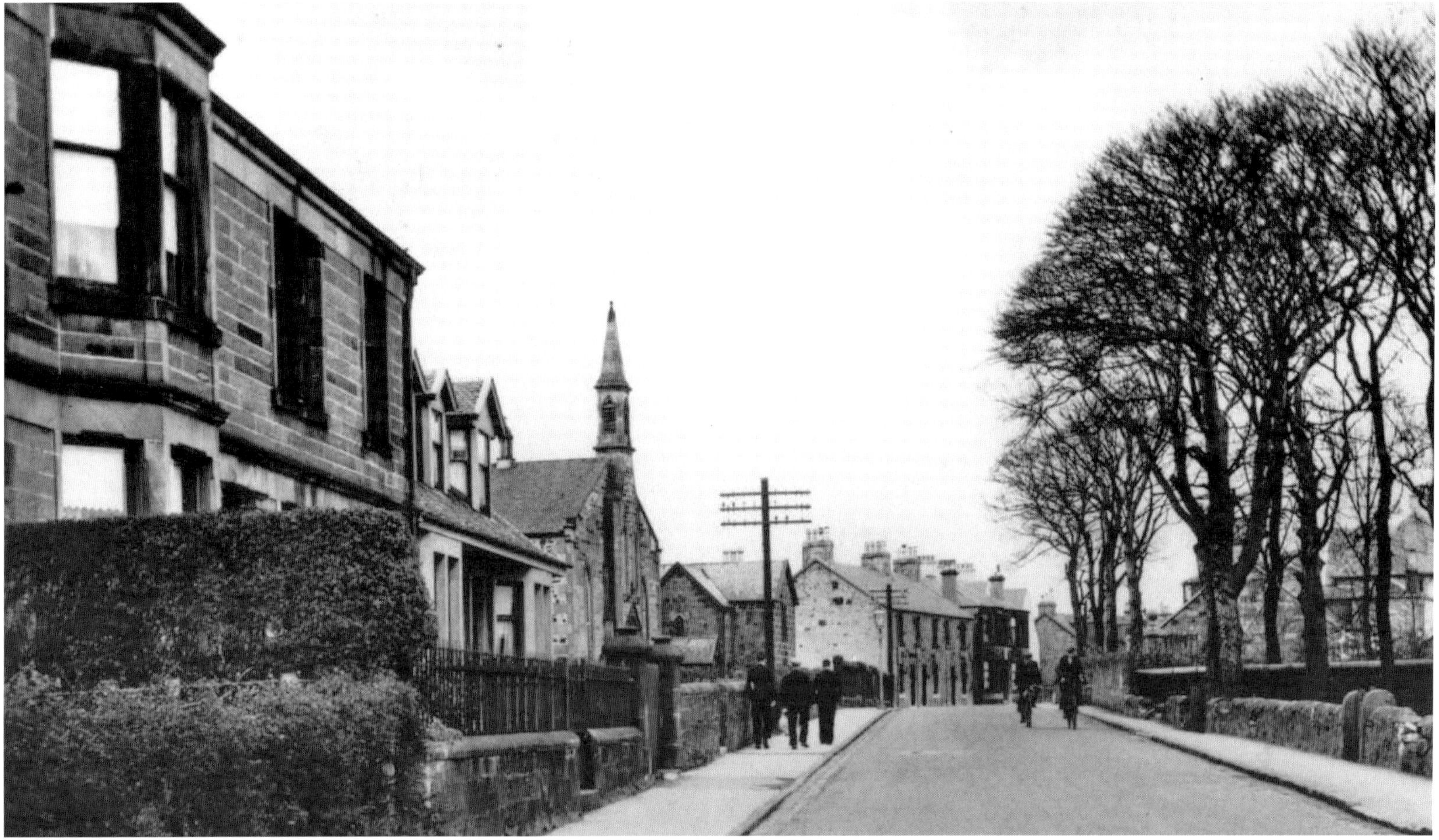

In this later view of Chryston Main Street, Chryston United Free Church and its adjoining church hall can be seen immediately to the right of West End Cottages. The church hall was opened in 1848 and during its lifetime was used as a day school in addition to its normal function. This ceased in 1877 when a new Board School was opened on Lindsaybeg Road. The church hall continued to simply function as such, until the church (then Chryston West Church) formed a union with Chryston East Church in 1950 to become Chryston Parish Church. At that time the church hall was demolished and the former United Free Church converted for use as a church hall for the new joint congregation. It, in turn, was demolished around 2002, when a new church hall was built within the grounds of the Parish Church. On the opposite side of Main Street the low stone wall to the right of photograph contains the entrance to the then parish church manse.

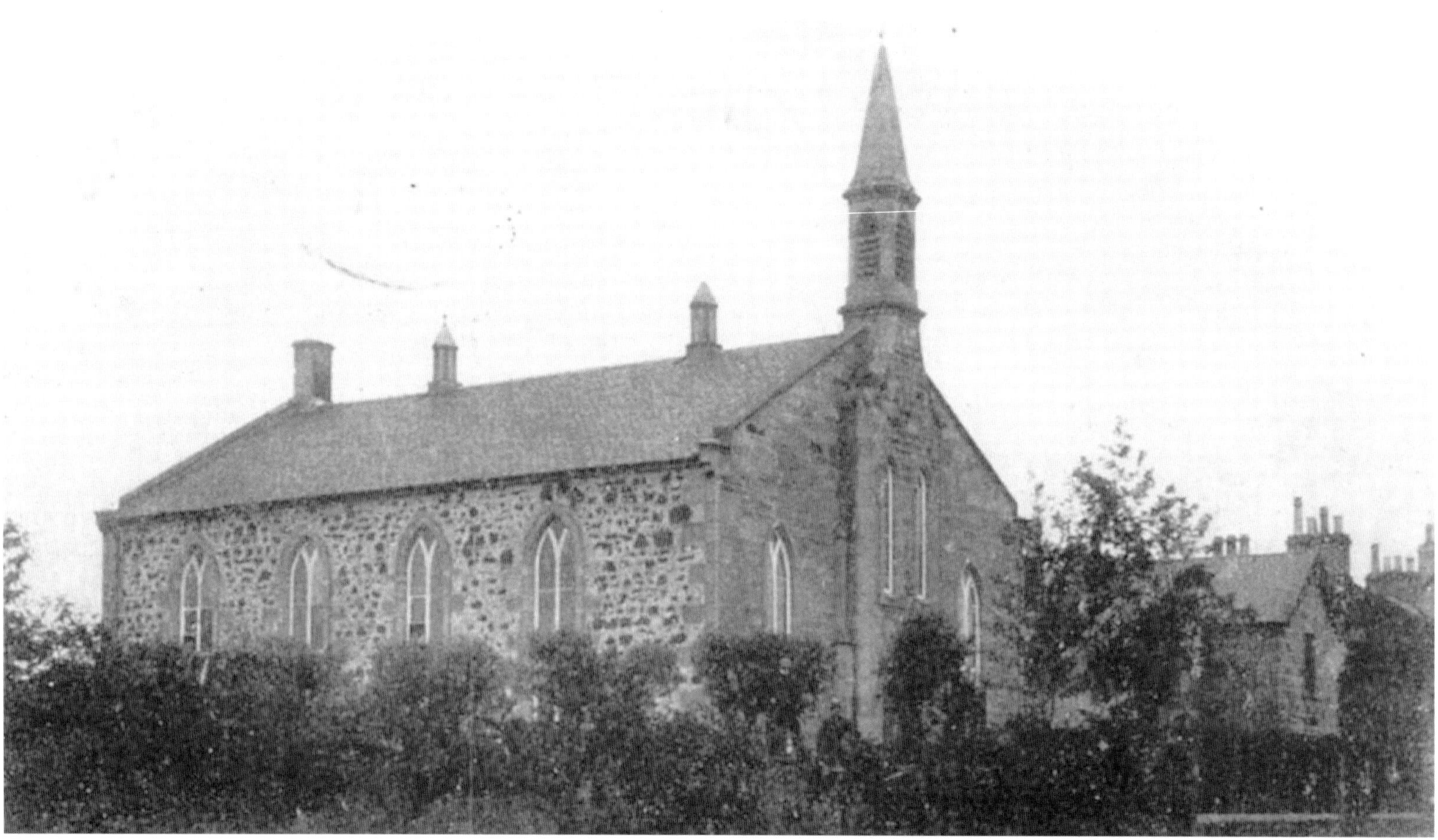

Like many other churches throughout Scotland, Chryston Free Church was formed during the Disruption in 1843 when some parish ministers and their congregations left the established church in protest against the then system of appointing ministers. The stone used in building this church was gifted by Alexander Campbell of Bedlay House and came from his Bedlay Quarry. It is reported that during the construction of the church, before an impending storm, the Free Church members felt compelled to temporarily secure the unfinished steeple with ropes, which caused much hilarity amongst the Parish Church members! Incorporated within the steeple was the so-called 'wakening bell', which was installed in the belfry in 1847. Forged in a Glasgow foundry, it was rung every Sunday at 9.00 a.m. until the outbreak of the Second World War. In 1900, when a majority of the Free and United Presbyterian churches in Scotland merged, the church was renamed Chryston United Free Church of Scotland. In 1929 there was a further change of name to Chryston West Church of Scotland, when the minister and the bulk of his congregation agreed to rejoin the established church.

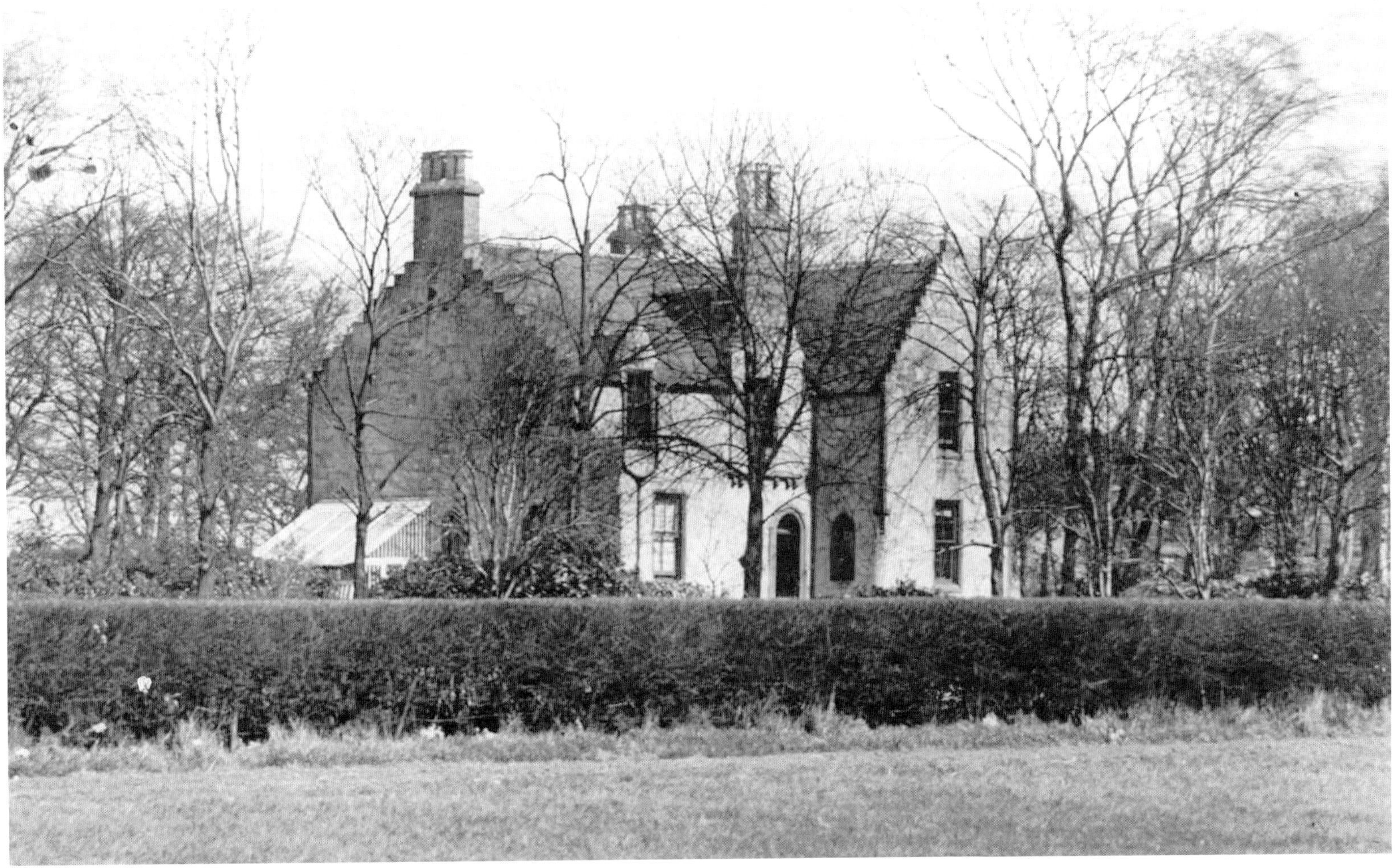

This substantial property, seen here around the time of the First World War, served as the manse of the former United Free Church. Its construction was paid for by its first minister, the Rev. William Burnett, and it was later gifted by him to the congregation. Situated on the south side of Main Street, at the western edge of Chryston, it was, when first built, surrounded on three sides by open fields. Following the union of the West and East Churches, the manse was deemed surplus to requirements and in 1952 was sold and renamed West House. It was later demolished and a new housing development, named Burnett Court in honour of this much-loved minister, was built on its site.

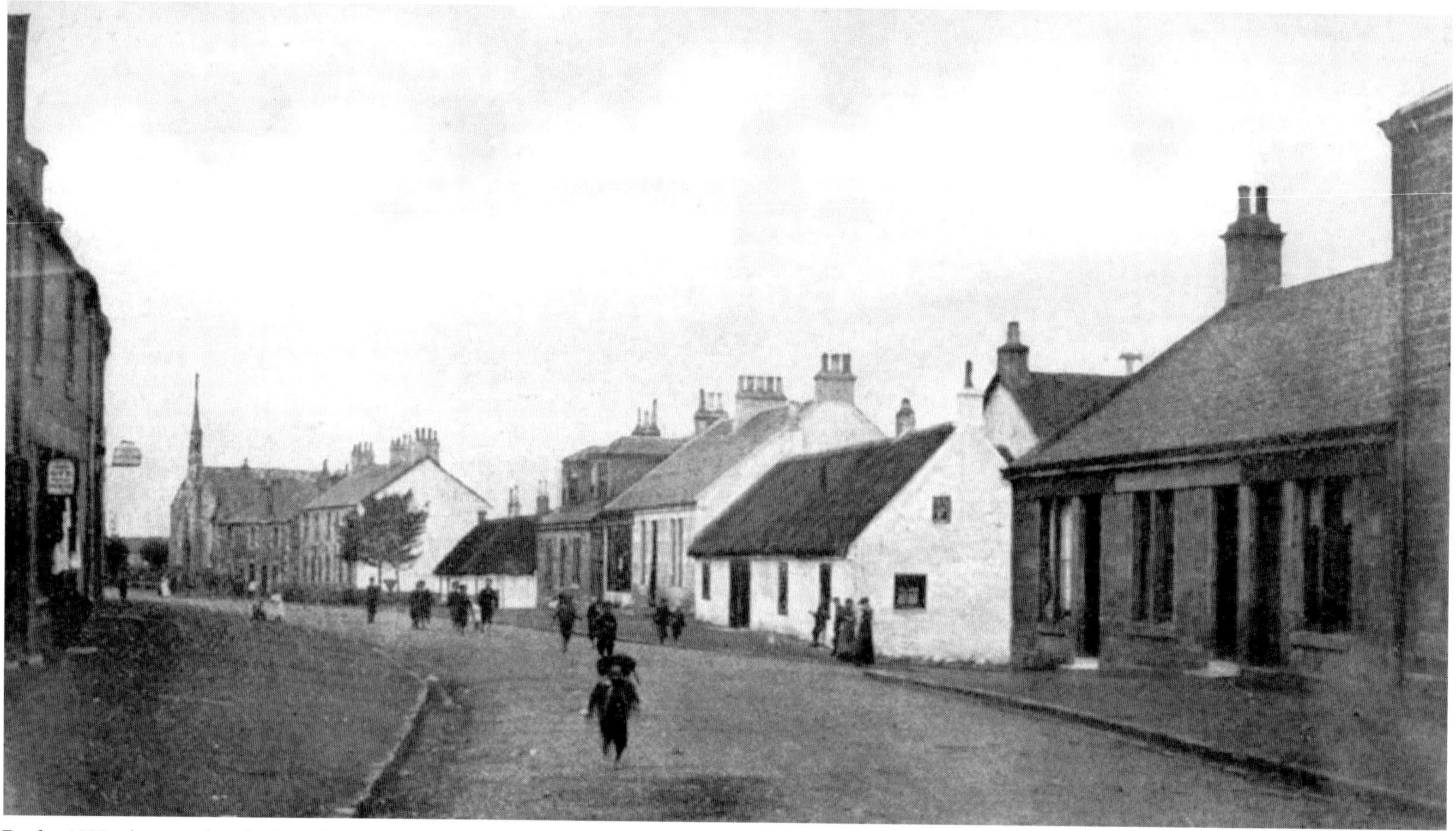

By the 1930s the two thatched-roofed cottages (seen here on the north side of Main Street, Chryston, to the west of Gartferry Road) had already gone. These were followed, from the 1960s onwards, by the buildings on the opposite side of the street and, in more recent times, by the Chryston United Free Church (seen here further down Main Street). The few present-day survivors include Dunollie (the single-storey property on the extreme right of photograph) and the single-storey property (known variously as Baxter's House and McCready's Building) to the left of the thatched cottage which is nearest the camera. From about 1938 to 1958, Dunollie was used as a grocery shop, operated by Coatbridge Co-operative Society. It is said that in the period following the Second World War, when rationing was in force, local parents would order their children to play in the vicinity of the store so that they could alert their parents to any deliveries of fresh fruit such as bananas! After the Co-op store closed, the rear of the premises was used as a blacksmith's workshop by Iain Carslaw, before being taken over in 1964 by plumbing and heating engineers Carter & Cowan. Dunollie is now a private house.

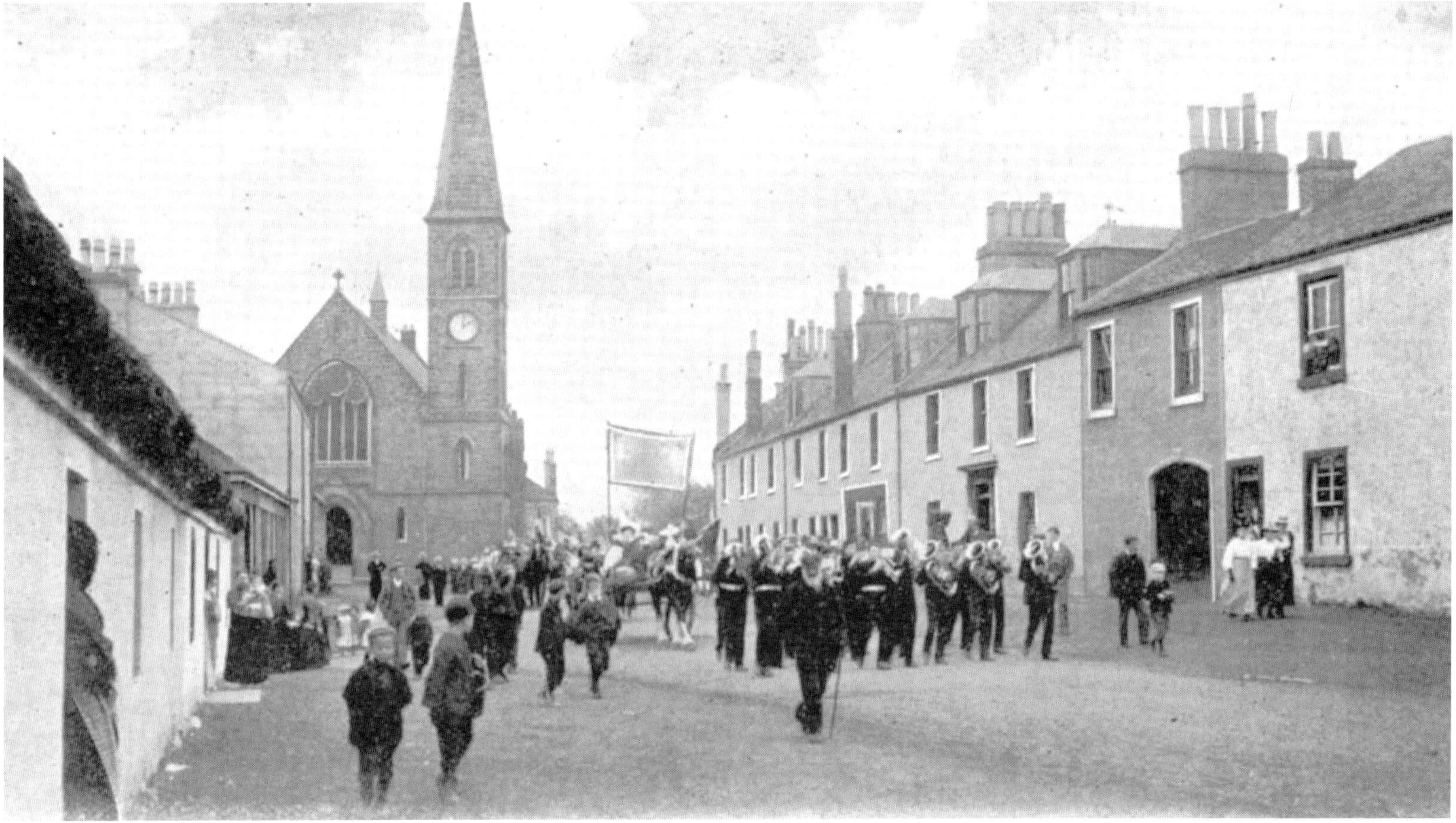

In this late 1890s view of Chryston Main Street, a procession headed by a local brass band is seen heading towards Cardowan. The participants, most probably on their annual Sunday school trip, are being transported on open farm carts drawn by massive Clydesdale horses. Such transport was usually provided by local farmers, who would also allow the use of their fields for games and races, in addition to providing milk to supplement the bags of eats (typically sandwiches, scones and cakes) supplied by the organisers. The only thing the picnickers were generally required to bring was a 'tinny' for their milk. Among the older properties on this stretch of Main Street is Alexander Barr's Chryston Inn (third building from the right, and distinguishable by its heavy door lintel). The arched pend alongside the inn led to stables at the rear of the building, while a door located immediately inside the pend, on the left, gave access to Baxter's Hall. This hall was located on the upper floor of the inn and was used for social events. Over the years, it also provided accommodation for local organisations such as the Masonic Lodge, the Orange Lodge, and the Salvation Army.

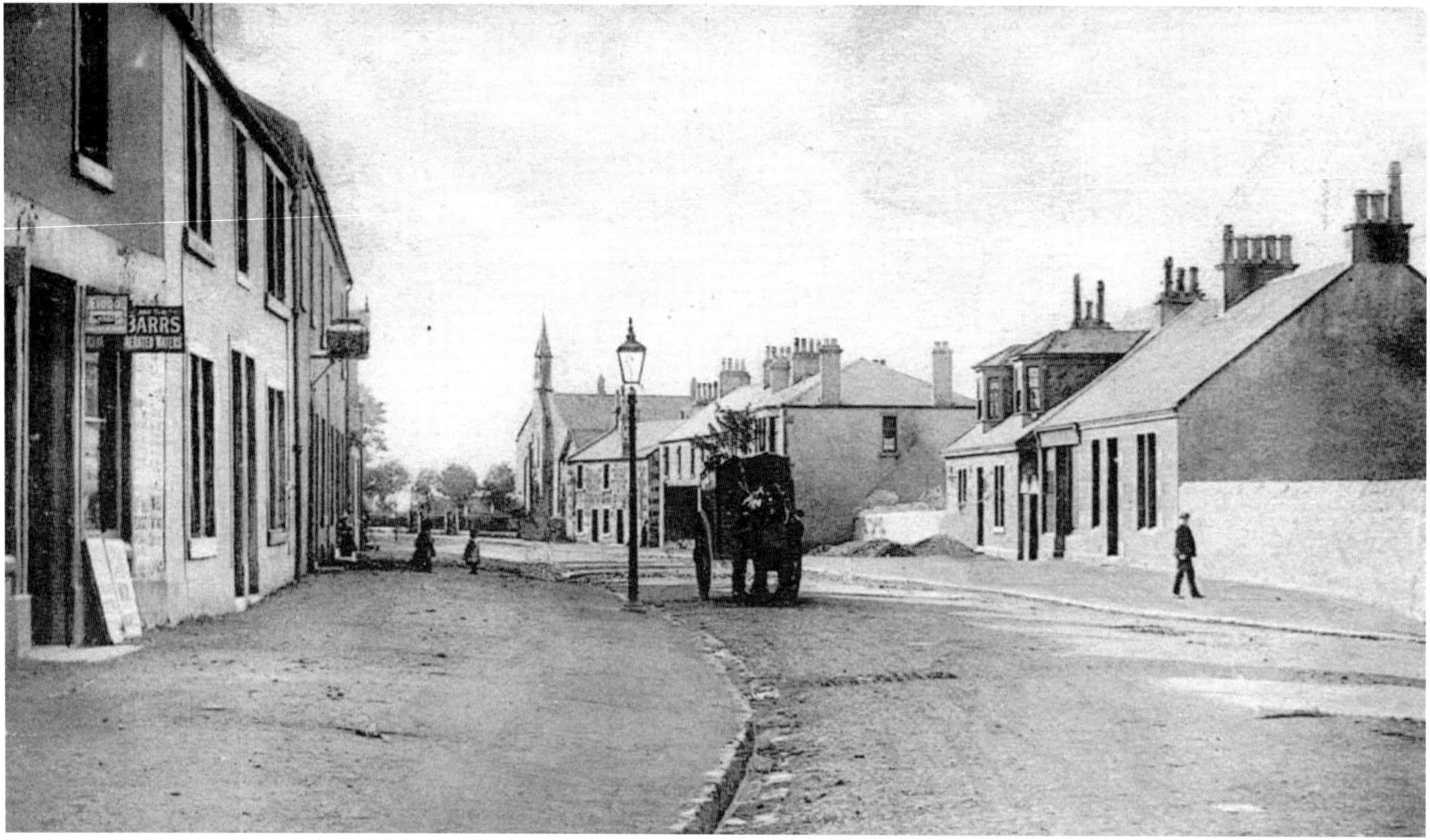

This early 1900s view of Chryston Main Street has been taken from just east of Gartferry Road, looking west. On the extreme left of photograph is William McMillan's drapery and grocery shop. Later owners of this property included MacPherson Brothers and E. & M. Anderson, both of whom also ran a grocery shop on the site. The building on the extreme right of photograph comprised both a house and a shop. Over the years the shop housed a tailor, a confectioner (which also sold home-made ice lollipops), an electrician, a butcher and, finally, a bakery. The tailor was the well-respected Archibald Baxter, who died in May 1939. Although a native of Chryston, he had trained in Saville Row in London, and, accordingly, was well-patronised by customers both near and far. Another equally distinguished local tailor was William Sheach. In 1912 he was reported as having invented an adjustable calculator which, it was claimed, was 'the most rapid mental calculator ever introduced into the science of cutting', and would be a 'boon' to tailors.

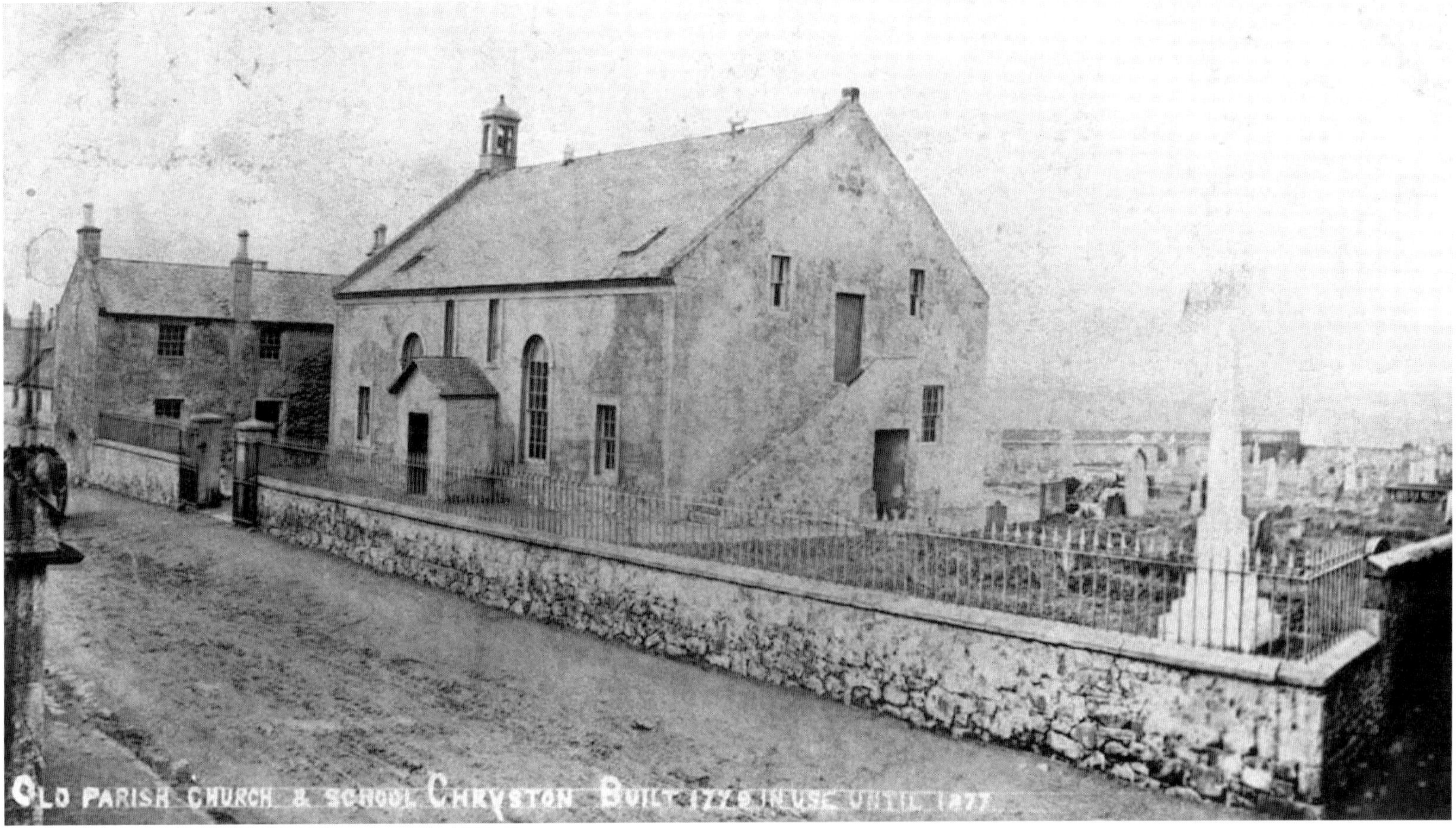

In the foreground of this 1906 view of Chryston Main Street is the Chryston Chapel of Ease, with the old parish school to its rear. This school was opened around 1782 and replaced a thatched-roof cottage which had been, in effect, Chryston's first school. In the 1820s the parish school was enlarged to provide accommodation for a teacher. Until that time the teacher stayed in a farmer's barn during the summer months and lodged free in the home of one of the pupils during winter. The Chryston Chapel of Ease was opened in 1780 on ground belonging to James Gray of Wamflet and could accommodate 450 persons. As was the custom at the time, income was initially largely accrued from seat rents, although several seats – designated 'Poor's Seats' – were available to people unable to afford to pay this rent. On 20 June 1870 the chapel was elevated to a *quoad sacra* parish church. Seven years later, following a final service held on 15 April 1877, the Chapel of Ease was demolished and replaced by the present-day Chryston Parish Church. The old parish school was also demolished at this time, but the chapel graveyard (which was closed to new burials in 1861), seen here to extreme right of photograph, has survived intact.

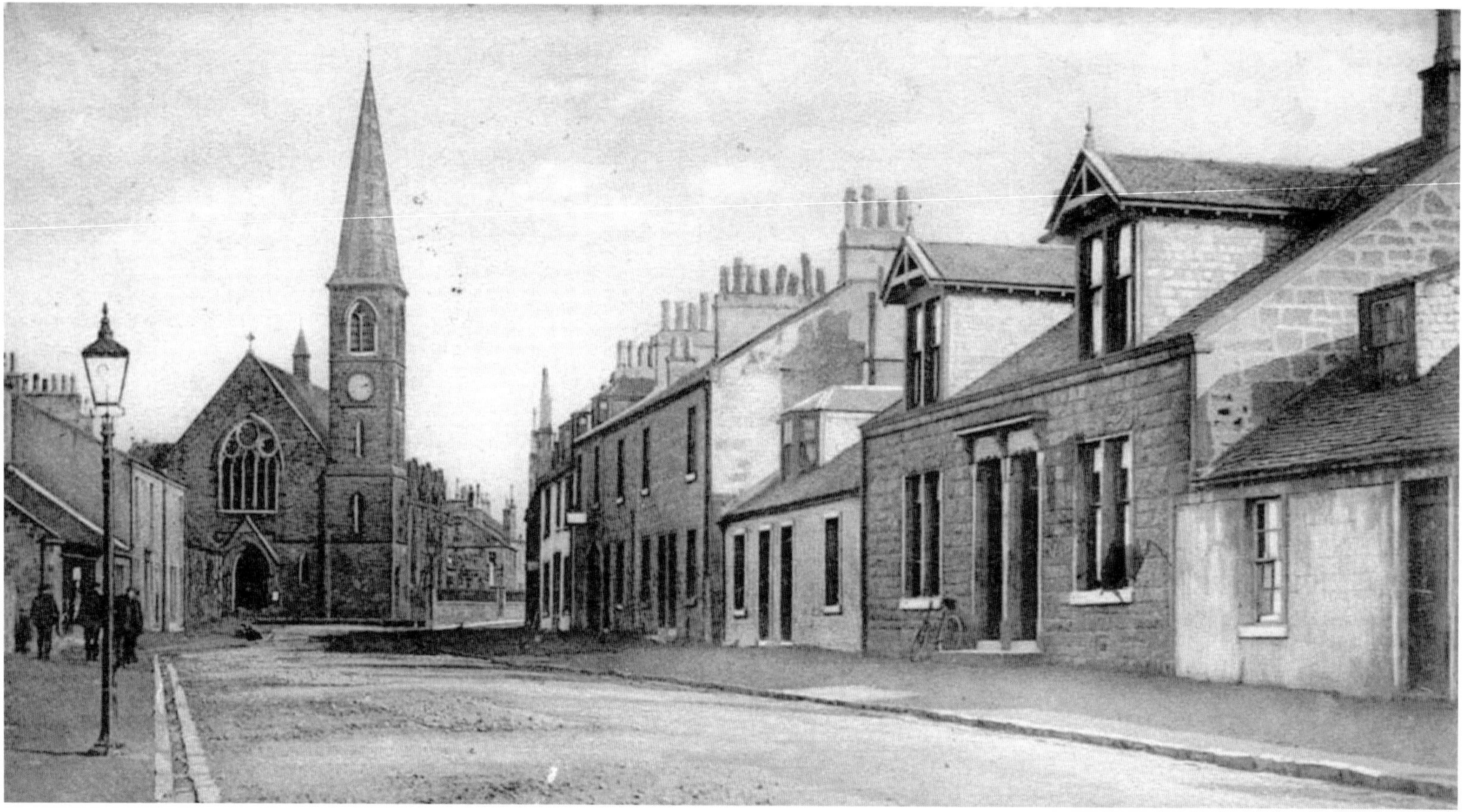

In this photograph, taken around 1913 and looking east, many of the older properties on both sides of Main Street can be seen. On the left of the picture, at the junction of Gartferry Road and Main Street (just past where the men are standing), is Dunollie and the two-storey tenement Ochil View. Just beyond is Chryston Parish Church. This church, which was designed by the Glasgow architectural firm of Thomson & Turnbull, was opened on 4 August 1878, and was capable of accommodating 800 worshippers. While the church was under construction, the congregation met in the newly opened Chryston Public School and later, briefly, in the Drill Hall in Muirhead. In 1929, when the United Free Church rejoined the established Church of Scotland, the parish church was renamed Chryston East Church. Finally, in 1950, when the East and West Churches merged, the East Church was retained as the church and reverted to the name of Chryston Parish Church. Among the older properties on the right-hand side of Main Street is a single-storey building with the single roof dormer (next to the two-storey property), which was bought by the Sutherland family after the last war. From this they ran a shop selling everything from sweets and toys to clothes. Further along the street is the Chryston Inn, distinguishable by its hanging sign.

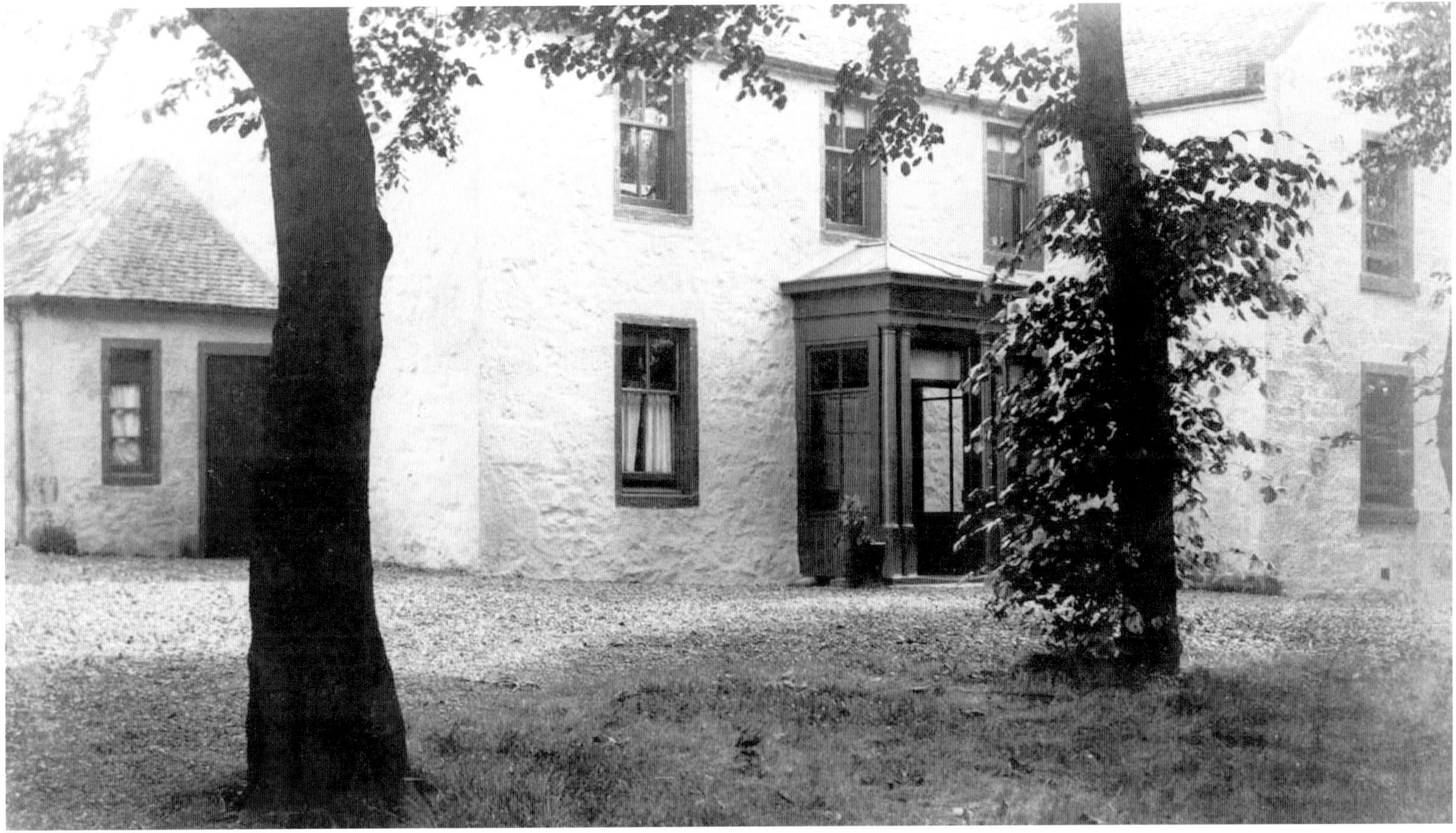

Part of the frontage of Chryston Parish Church manse can be seen in this photograph taken in 1909. The manse, the foundation stone of which was laid in 1803, faces onto Chryston Main Street. It is now a private residence and, externally at least, appears largely unchanged today. Undoubtedly one of the manse's most colourful occupants was the Rev. James Young, who lived there alone from 1819 until 1852. A much-loved, if somewhat eccentric, minister, it was said that he was often to be found at home 'studying his bible seated on a stool by a miserable fire and encased in newspapers as part of his outer clothing'. In 1955, shortly after the union of the East and West Churches, the manse was sold. Ardenvohr, a private house at the head of Potassels Road in Muirhead, was then used as the manse. This new manse had been the residence of the Jackson family, the last of whom was Margaret Jane Haldane Jackson, a daughter of George Craig Murphy who ran the nearby post office and grocery shop for many years. In 1977, when a new purpose-built manse was erected within the parish church grounds, Ardenvohr was sold and reverted once more to being a private residence.

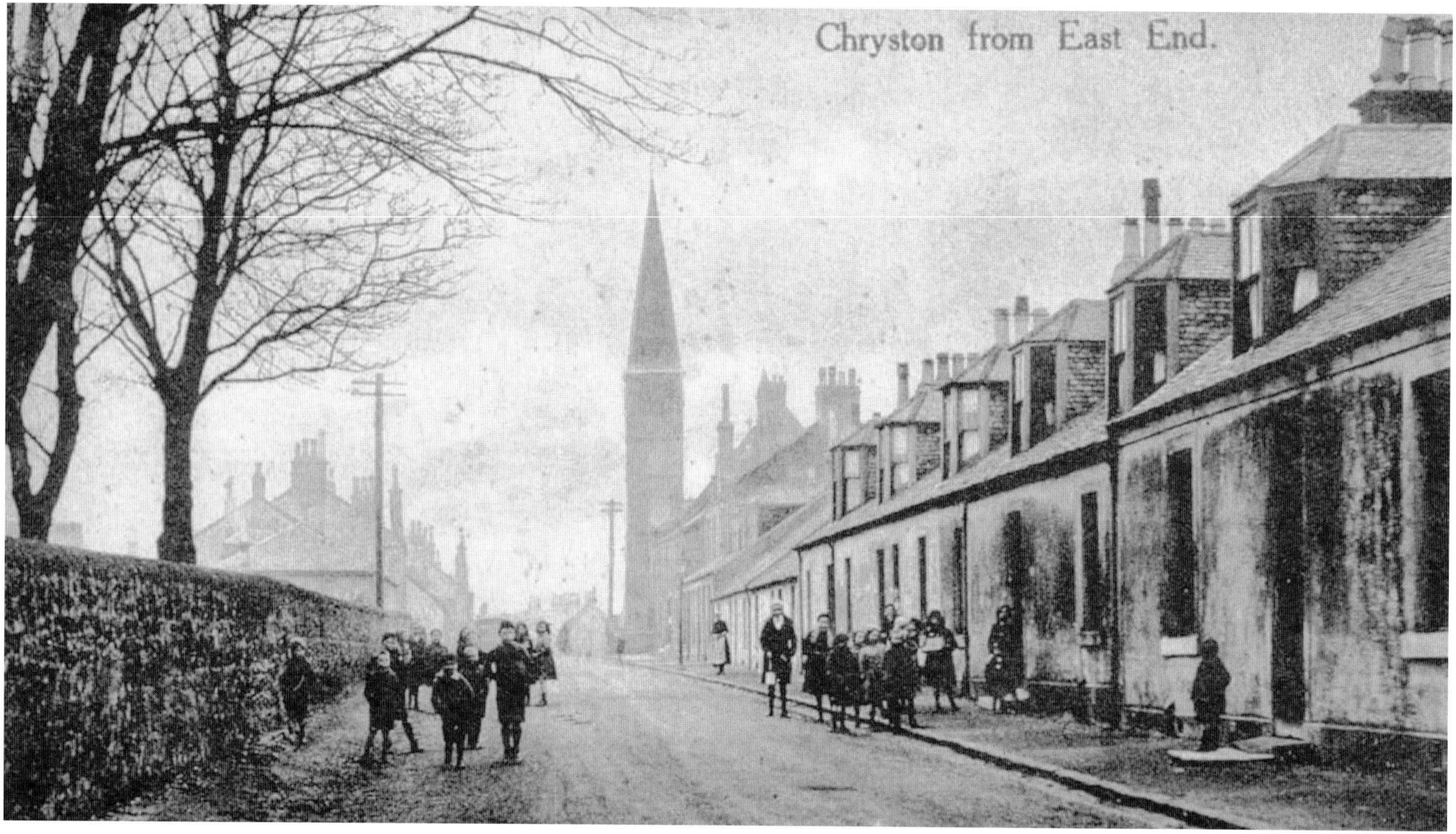

In this early view of Chryston East End, looking west, can be seen the older properties on the north side of Main Street up to the parish church. These include Millbrae Terrace (nearest the camera), followed by Knox Land and Kirk Place. Although mostly residential, the property with the roof dormers (just beyond the lady wearing the white apron) was, around 1901, Jane Ogilvie's grocery and hardware shop. Also here, circa 1921, was a confectionery shop operated by Mrs Margaret Davis who reputedly also sold hot mushy peas! Next door to Mrs Davis's shop, for a period from the 1920s until the 1950s, was Alexander McDonald's cobbler's shop. Known locally as 'Mac the Cobbler', he was also a proficient musician who, it was said, could play a fine tune using a wood saw and a poker! Mac was succeeded by cobbler Tommy Wales, who could often be found with a mouthful of tacks, working on heavy miners' boots. Later, the shop was converted by local boxer Nicky McGuire into a boxing booth for up and coming young boxers. To the left of the photograph, behind the high stone wall, was a field used by nearby Chryston Mains Farm.

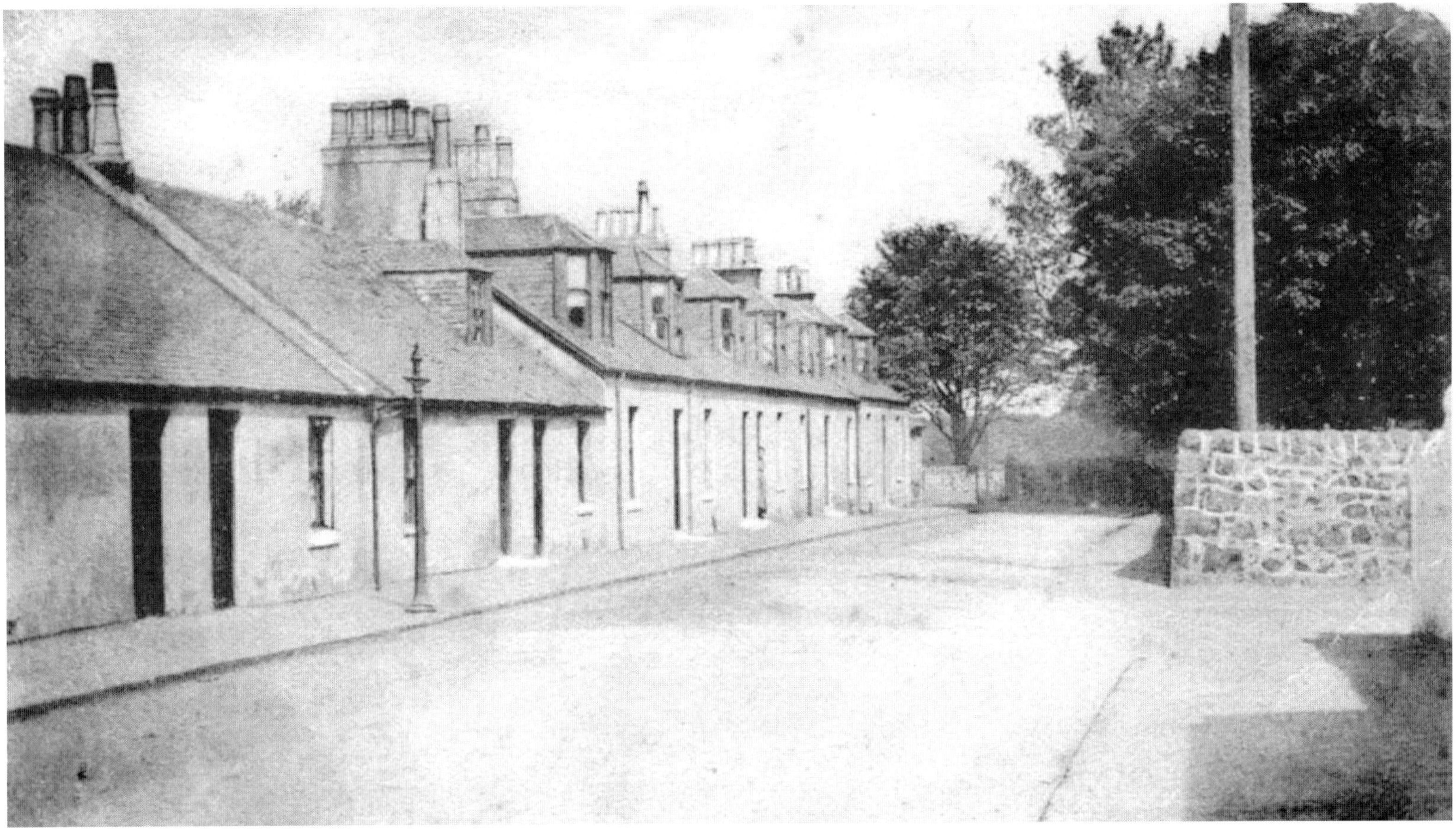

This early view, taken at the East End of Chryston (at the head of Chryston Road) and looking east, shows some of the village's early nineteenth-century weavers' cottages. The weavers – who also worked seasonally on the farms – initially produced good quality linen cloth from locally grown flax, but later progressed to cotton cloth when the market for linen declined. The most celebrated of these local weavers was Walter Watson, the so-called 'Poet Laureate of Chryston', who is buried in the old graveyard attached to the former Chapel of Ease. A granite obelisk in his memory, erected by public subscription in 1873, stands near his grave. Beyond the cottages, the road swings to the left towards Millbrae House and the McGregor family's Millbrae Nurseries. For many years this nursery was heated by gas which seeped out of the ground at various spots within Bedlay Glen. This phenomenon was also said to provide a constant source of amusement for local children who, on finding pockets of escaping gas at the edge of the burn, would ignite the gas with lit matches, thereby giving the illusion of setting the burn alight!

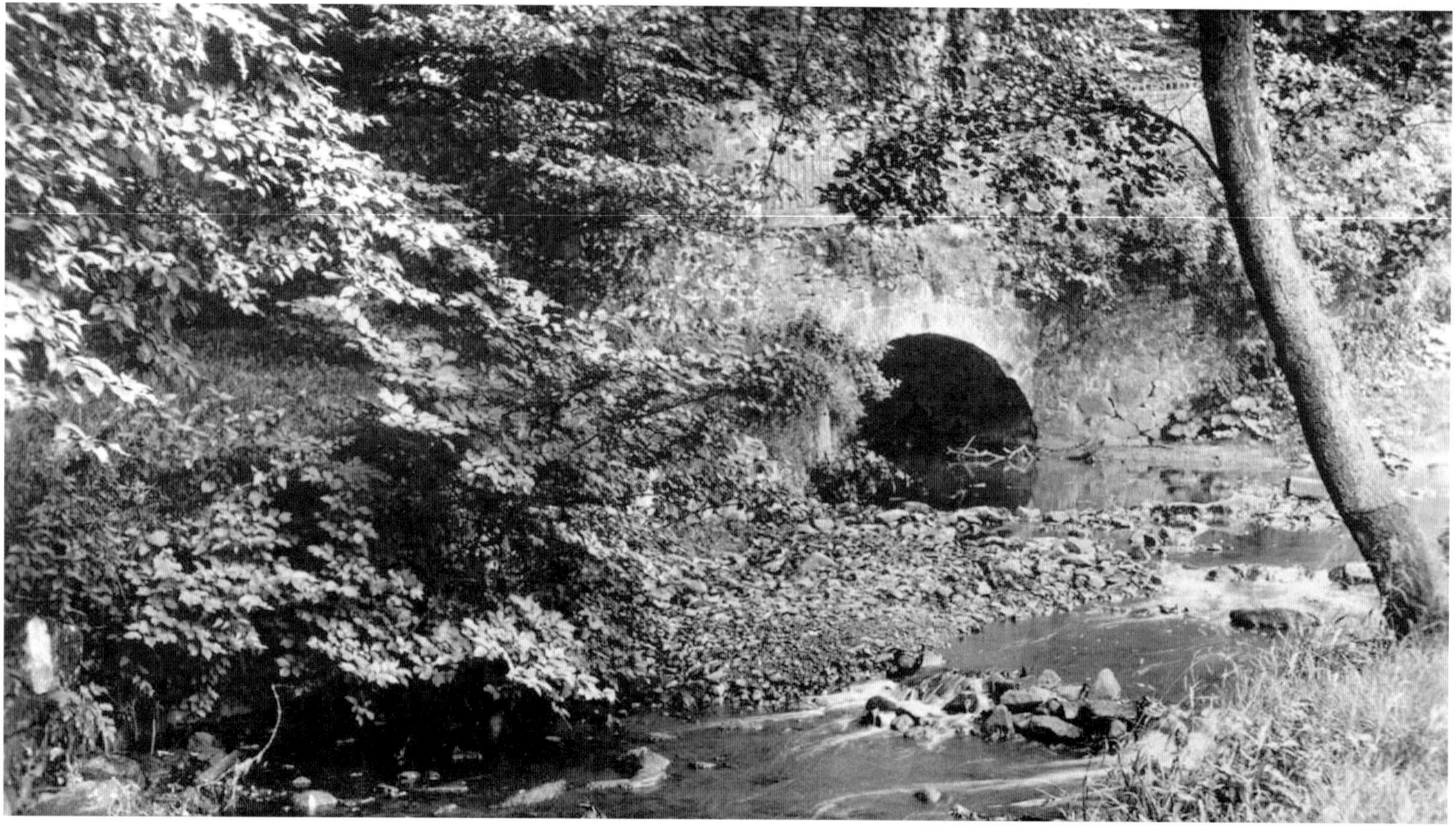

Shortly after it enters Bedlay Glen, the Bothlyn Burn flows under this nineteenth-century stone bridge, which forms part of a long-standing local right-of-way known as the Well Brae path. The right-of-way (formerly the main route heading to, or coming from, the east) cuts through the grounds of Bedlay Castle and in the first half of the 1800s the Campbell family, the then owners of the estate, twice tried (unsuccessfully) to deny villagers access to it. These attempts were fiercely resisted, since the right-of-way gave access to Bedlay Well. This well, which was first used around 1760, was the most used of several wells in the vicinity and, according to local lore, was used by no less a personage than Bonnie Prince Charlie! Although the water drawn from the well was said by villagers to be far superior to that later supplied by Glasgow Corporation, there were times when the well was so dry that even a smallish container could take hours to fill. Although long since abandoned, the well's location is easily identified, as the stone slab, which covers the stairs leading down to the well, is still in position.

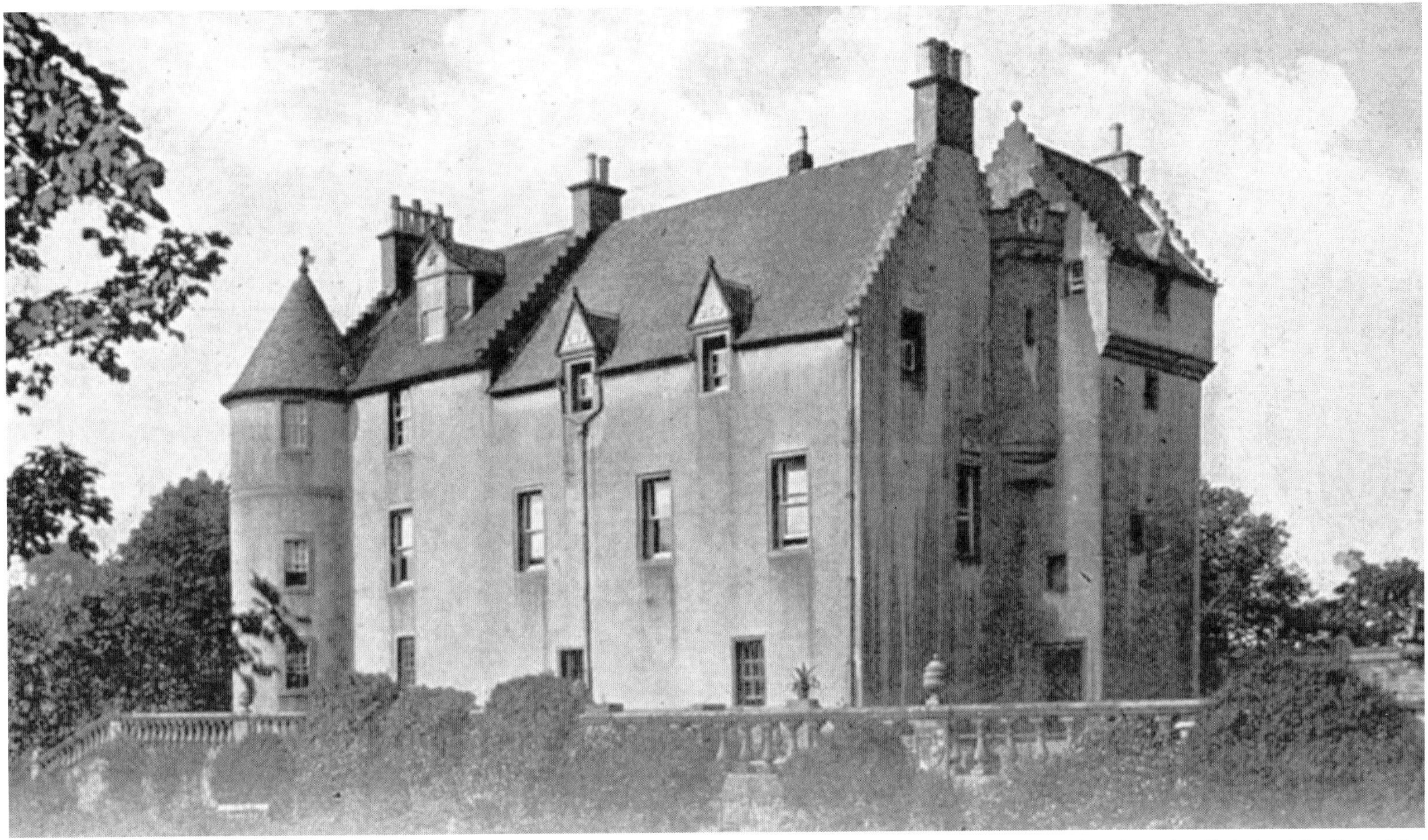

In 1854 the Bedlay Estate, including this fine sixteenth-century house, passed through marriage from the Campbell family to the Christies. The first of the Christie family to own the estate was Thomas Craig Christie, who carried out various improvements to the house and gardens. Unlike his immediate predecessors, Christie permitted locals and visitors free access to the estate. Prominent in local affairs, he served on various public bodies as Deputy Lieutenant of Lanarkshire, a justice of the peace, and a county councillor. After his death the estate passed to his youngest son, Walter Cross Buchanan Christie, who also served as a county councillor. On Walter's death in 1941 the estate was jointly inherited by his four sisters, Katherine, Eveline, Anna and Jean, none of whom married and all of whom lived to a ripe old age. The last of the family to survive was Jean Christie who, like her father, brother and sisters, was very active in local affairs. On Jean's death in 1958, the estate was acquired by Alexander McAdam.

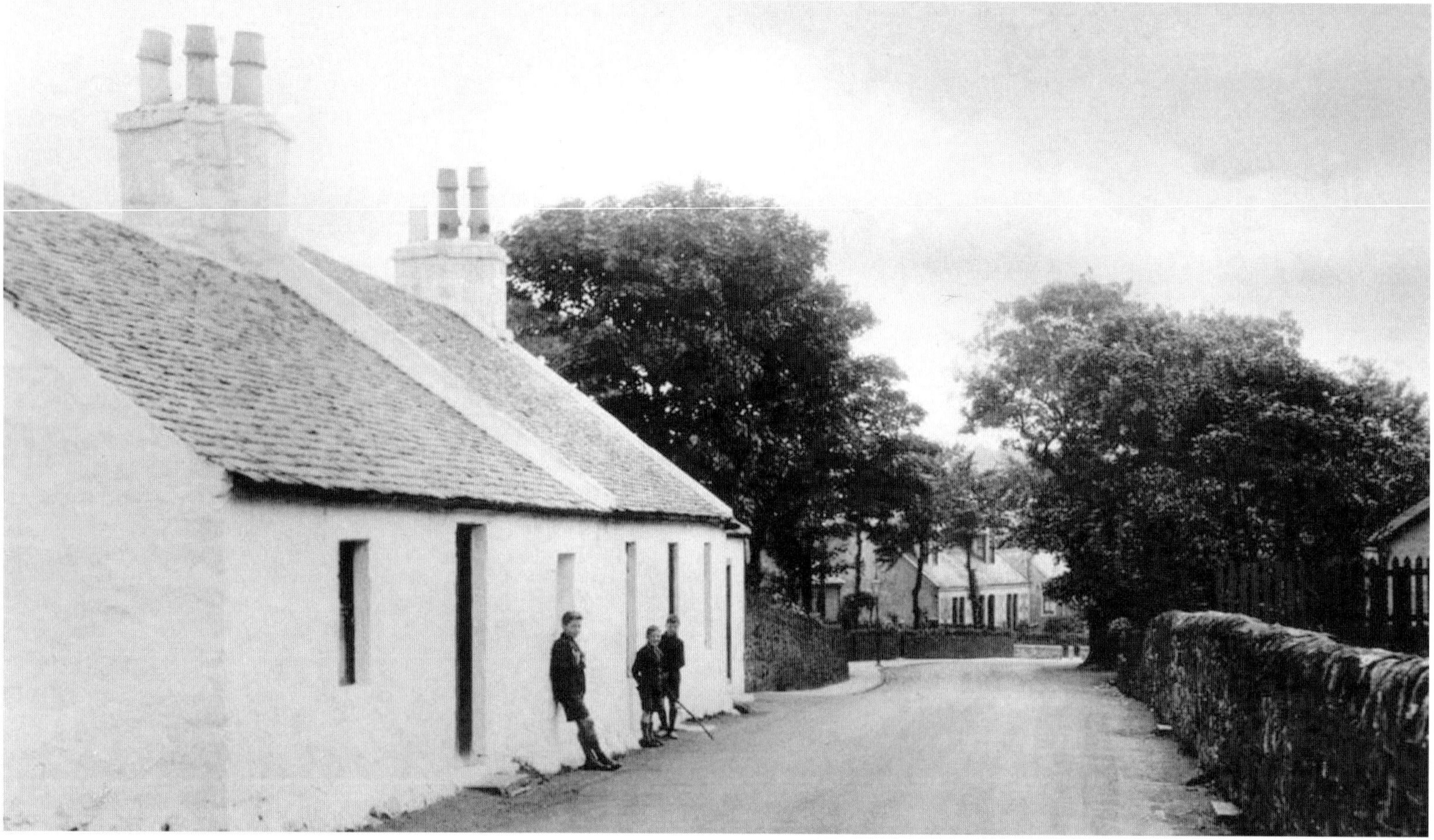

In this 1930s view, looking south from the head of Chryston Road, the single-storey whitewashed cottages known locally as Christie's Cottages can be seen to the left. Now demolished, these had provided accommodation for retired servants who had worked on the Bedlay Estate. The houses which can be seen further down Chryston Road, named Bothlyn and Linthrathen, still survive. On the opposite side of the road the stone wall marks the eastern boundary of Chryston Mains Farm. Originally known as Close Farm, this was in the hands of the Grays of Chryston for almost 300 years. From the late 1890s until the break up of the Garnkirk Estate in 1925, the tenancy was held by James Jackson and thereafter by Matthew Jackson Moffat (until his death in 1941). In 1974 the farm was sold by Matthew's widow, Margaret, and the farmhouse converted into a private residence. Despite several attempts to renovate the property, it was not until 1993 that a complete renovation was successfully carried out by the present owners.

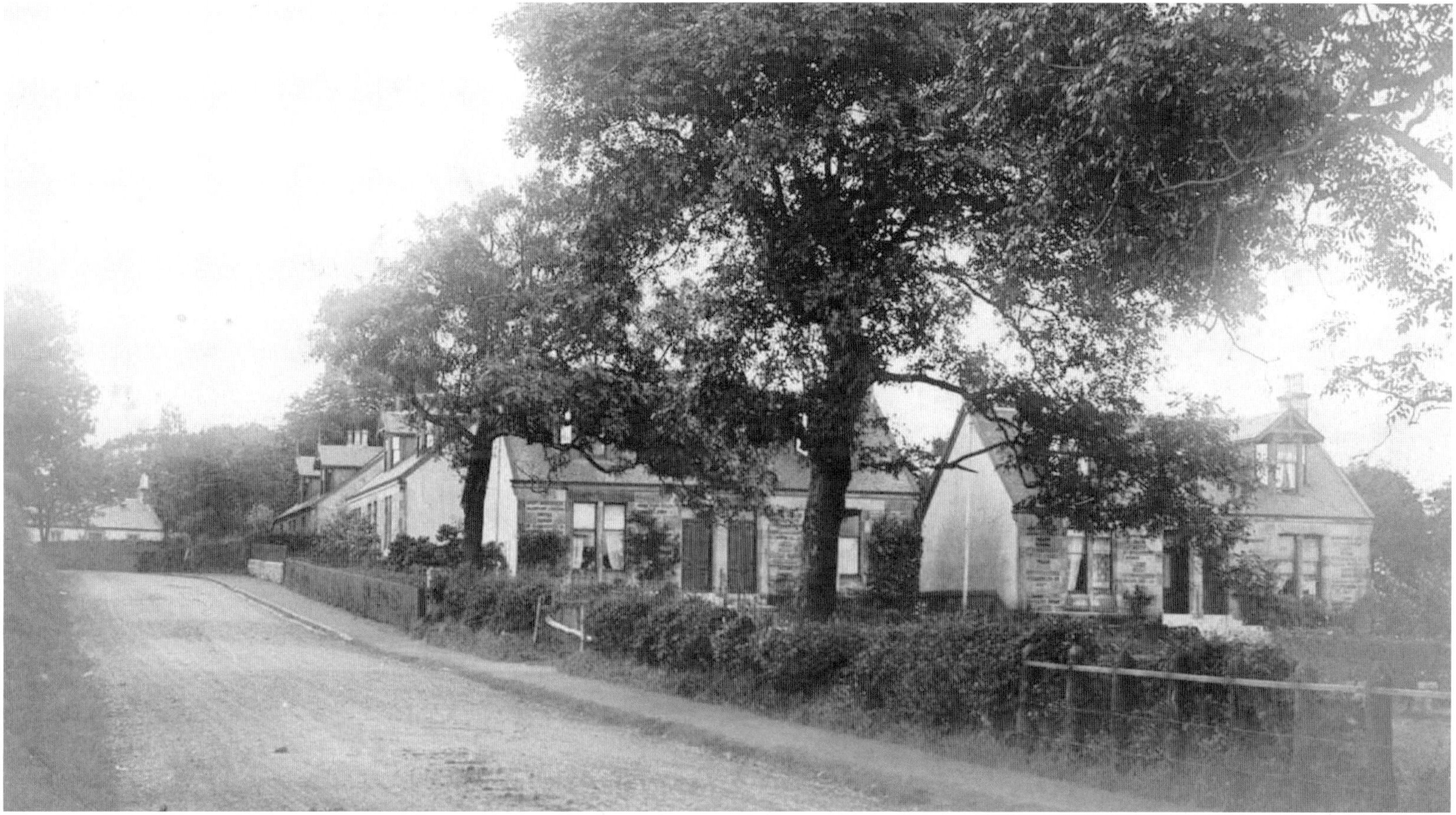

Seen here in this view of Chryston Road from around 1910, these two semi-detached properties facing the camera are among the oldest in Chryston. Situated on South Loan, the houses were built over a hundred years ago and today their appearance externally remains largely unchanged. Early residents of South Loan (though not necessarily of the cottages pictured) included local church elders Donald Munro and James Faulds, both of whom had a long-standing association with the 1st Chryston Boys' Brigade. In 1930 Donald, who had been an officer in the company since 1902, was honoured for his lengthy service, while James, who was captain when the company was formed in October 1897, was honoured with a plaque when a new Boys' Brigade hall was opened on Main Street in 1975. A common sight on the Loan (until the break-up of the farm in 1974) was cattle being herded between nearby Chryston Mains Farm and grazing fields further down Chryston Road. Initially, milk and buttermilk produced on the farm was sold around the doors but, after 1925, it was processed outside the district before being returned for sale within the Main Street dairy, latterly run by John and Jean Nisbet.

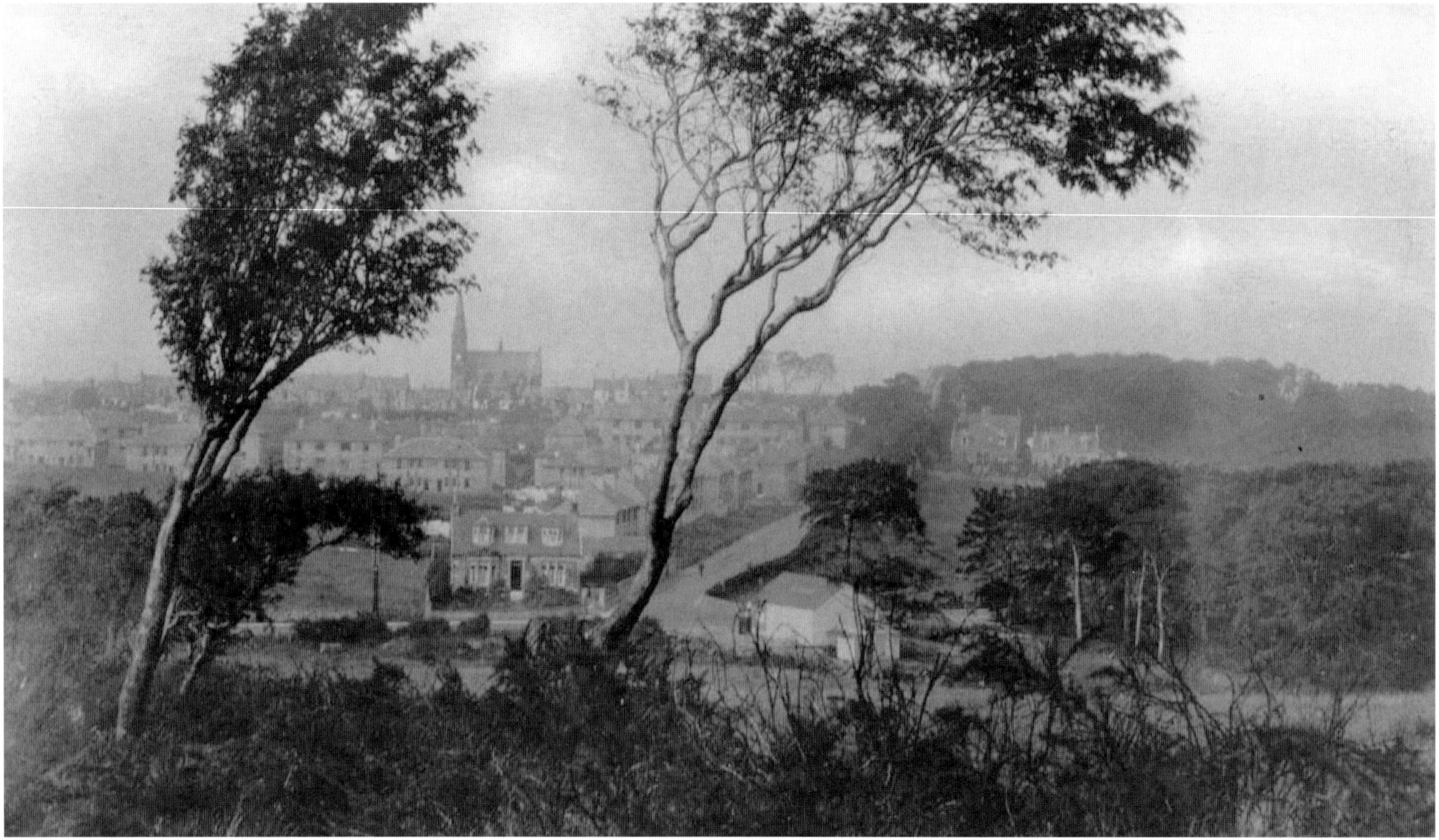

This view was taken from Lees Walk in the early 1920s, looking towards the then recently completed Hillcrest council housing scheme. The walk, which is believed to take its name from one of the occupants of nearby Glaudhall House, was also known as lovers' walk. It ran from the foot of Chryston Road at the rear of Braeside Garage (the white building in the foreground with the single petrol pump) to Drumcavel Road, although the more adventurous could continue on to Mount Ellen and Gartcosh. This popular walk was particularly well used by locals during the summer months, but less so in winter when it was prone to flooding. However, when winter snow covered the steep fields bordering the walk it became a means to an end for sledging enthusiasts – although this pastime appears to have been not without its dangers, as local newspapers record several instances of broken limbs and fatalities due to the steepness of the slopes. The villa in the foreground, with three roof dormers, is Cliffvale.

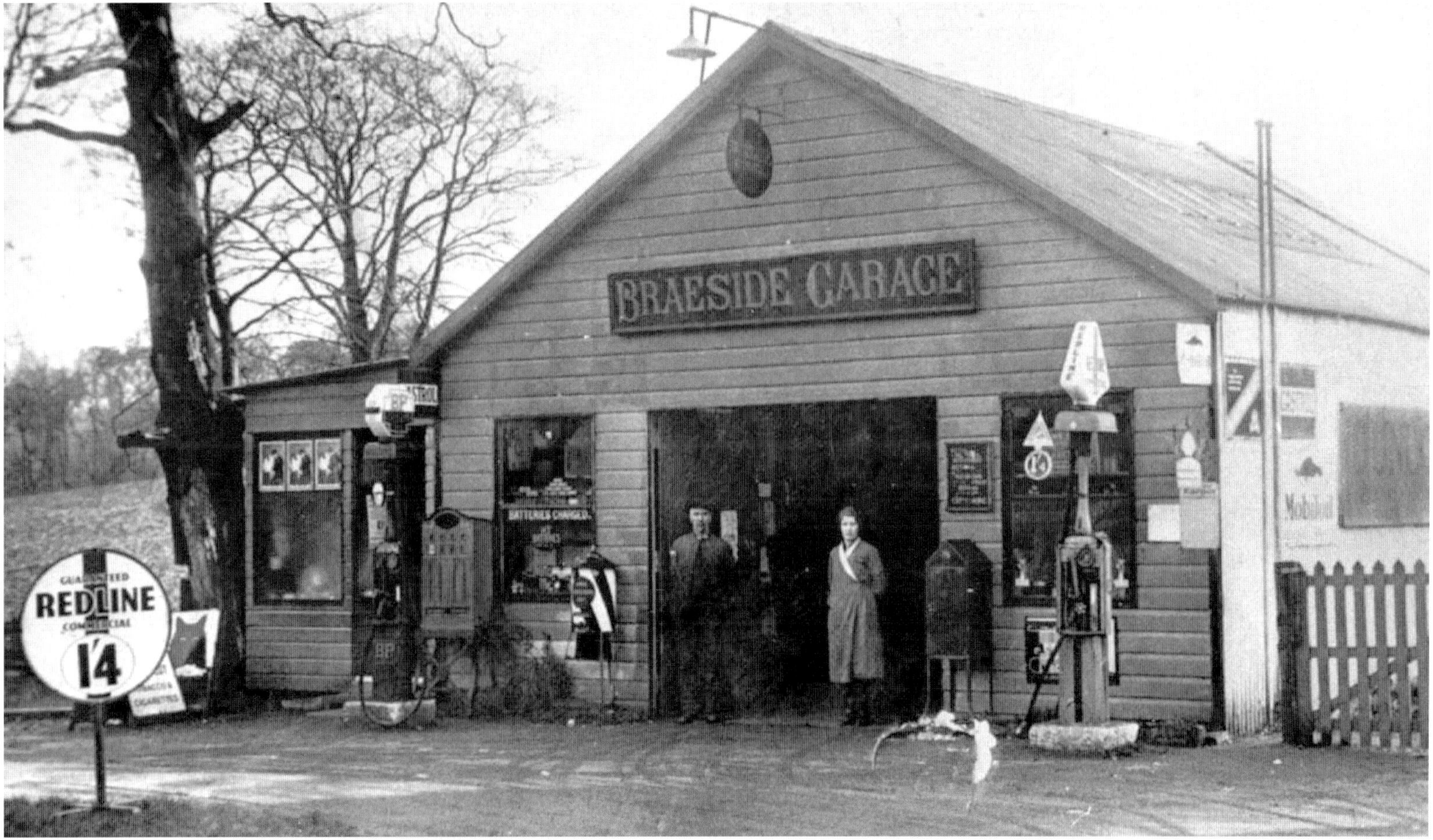

This 1930s photograph is of William Drummond's Braeside Garage, which was strategically sited on the main Glasgow–Stirling Road. In addition to filling up with Red Line petrol at 1s. 4d. (approximately 7p!) per gallon, and having car repairs done, local residents would also bring their radio accumulators to the garage for recharging. Later owners of the garage included Johnny Sword and his wife (who also operated a local car hire service, principally to transport school children staying in outlying areas) and John Cook, who took over the garage in the late 1970s. The latter, who resided on Cumbernauld Road, in the immediate vicinity of the garage, had previously been an engineer in nearby Bedlay Colliery. Under his ownership, the garage was rebuilt in its present form, incorporating an old Second World War air raid shelter. Although the garage also sold a small selection of groceries and sweets while under the ownership of both Drummond and Cook, this facility was greatly enhanced in 2007 when a dedicated Spar Store was opened within the garage.

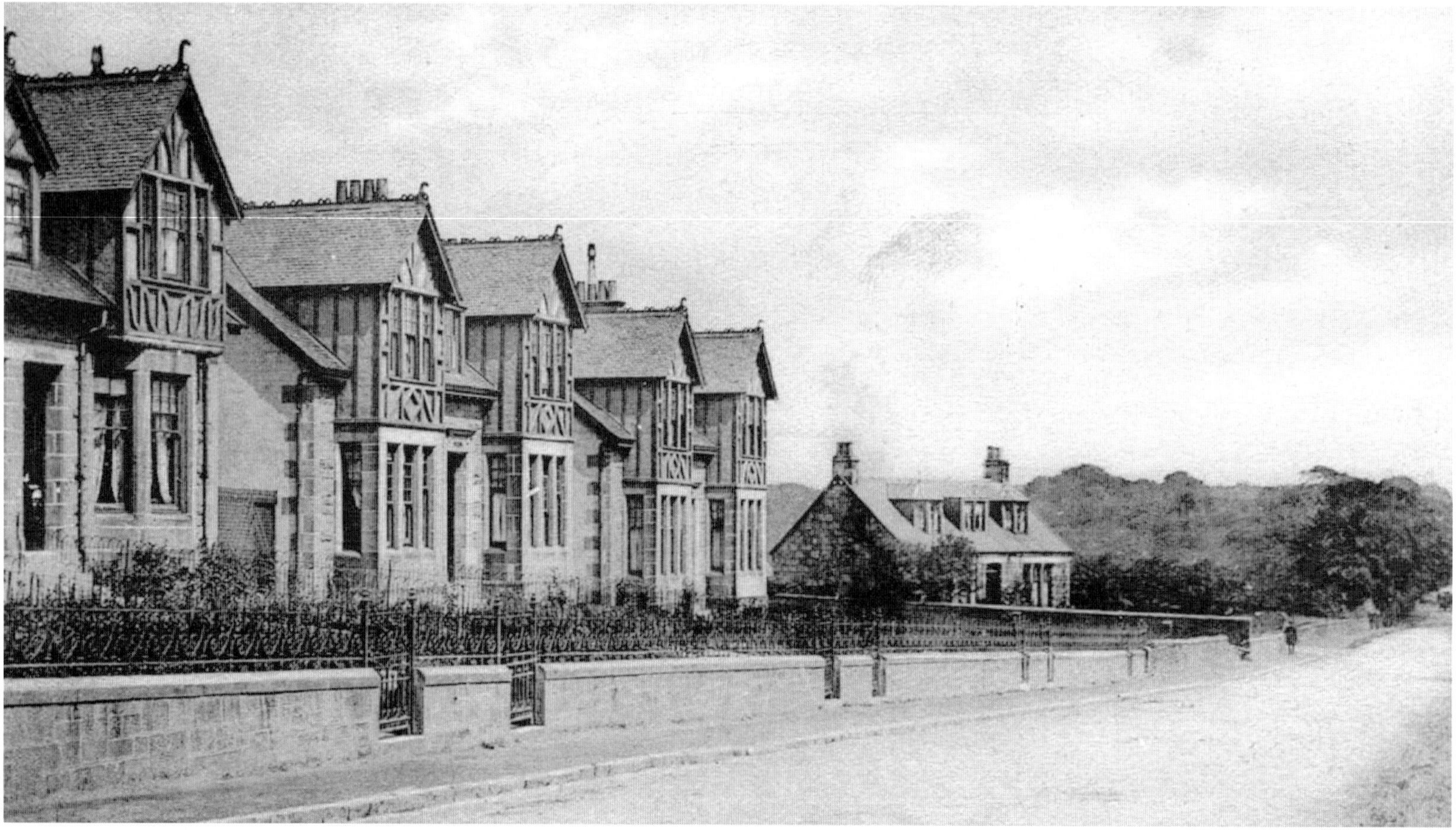

This view of Muirhead, looking east, shows some of the group of four matching semi-detached mock-Tudor style villas situated on the north side of Cumbernauld Road. Dating from around the turn of the twentieth century, the villas are thought to have been the work of local builders Messrs Allan Bros., Watson & Henderson. The villa on the extreme left of photograph is Craignure, which at one time was the residence of the Misses Clark-Murphy – this may explain why these properties are sometimes referred to locally as Murphy's Cottages. Next to Craignure is Cleveden, which at one time was occupied by William Fraser, the Coke Oven Manager at Auchengeich Colliery. Next again is Thirlestane. This villa was let to Cardowan Colliery (and its successor, the National Coal Board) for use by senior management. The detached cottage to the right of the villas, at Graham's Corner, has been known variously as Bellaville, Cliffvale and, presently, Springfield. For many years, this was the residence of Thomas Graham of the well-known Glasgow builders and plumbers merchants, Thomas Graham & Son. Graham, who died in 1944, was a popular figure in the area and took a keen interest in public affairs.

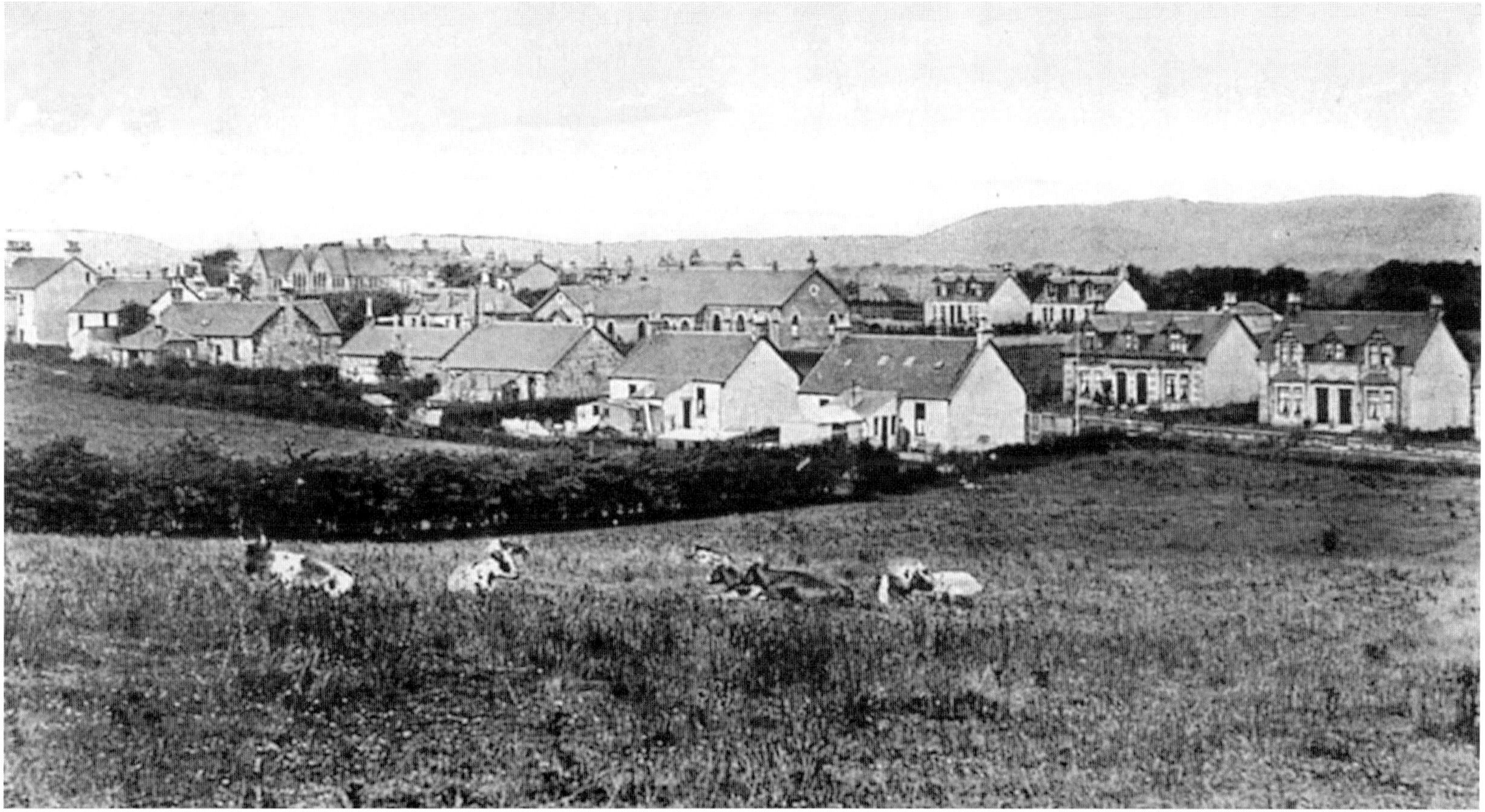

This 1905 view of Muirhead, taken from the open fields to the south of the village, shows the Drill Hall behind the cottages in the centre of the photograph, Chryston Public School in the left background, and some of the older properties on Cumbernauld Road. The Chryston Drill and Public Hall (to give it its full name) was opened in 1878, and in the beginning also served as a base for 'F' Company of the 7th Lanarkshire Rifle Volunteers (hence, presumably, its name). Initially, it was run by trustees who, some twenty years later, handed it over to Cadder Parish Council. At that time a lesser hall – the so-called 'new' hall – was built onto the south-facing gable wall of the original red brick structure, and its name changed to Muirhead Public Hall. Since then, various alterations have been made, including the construction of a new entrance, cloakrooms, and the addition of an annexe on the north side. In 1923 further alterations were required to the area in front of the building to enable the erection of a war memorial. This memorial was formally unveiled on 13 October 1923 by Lord Lamington, Depute Lord Lieutenant of the County of Lanark. Over the years the Hall has been used for a wide variety of community activities, including dances, concerts, picture shows, presentations and flower shows.

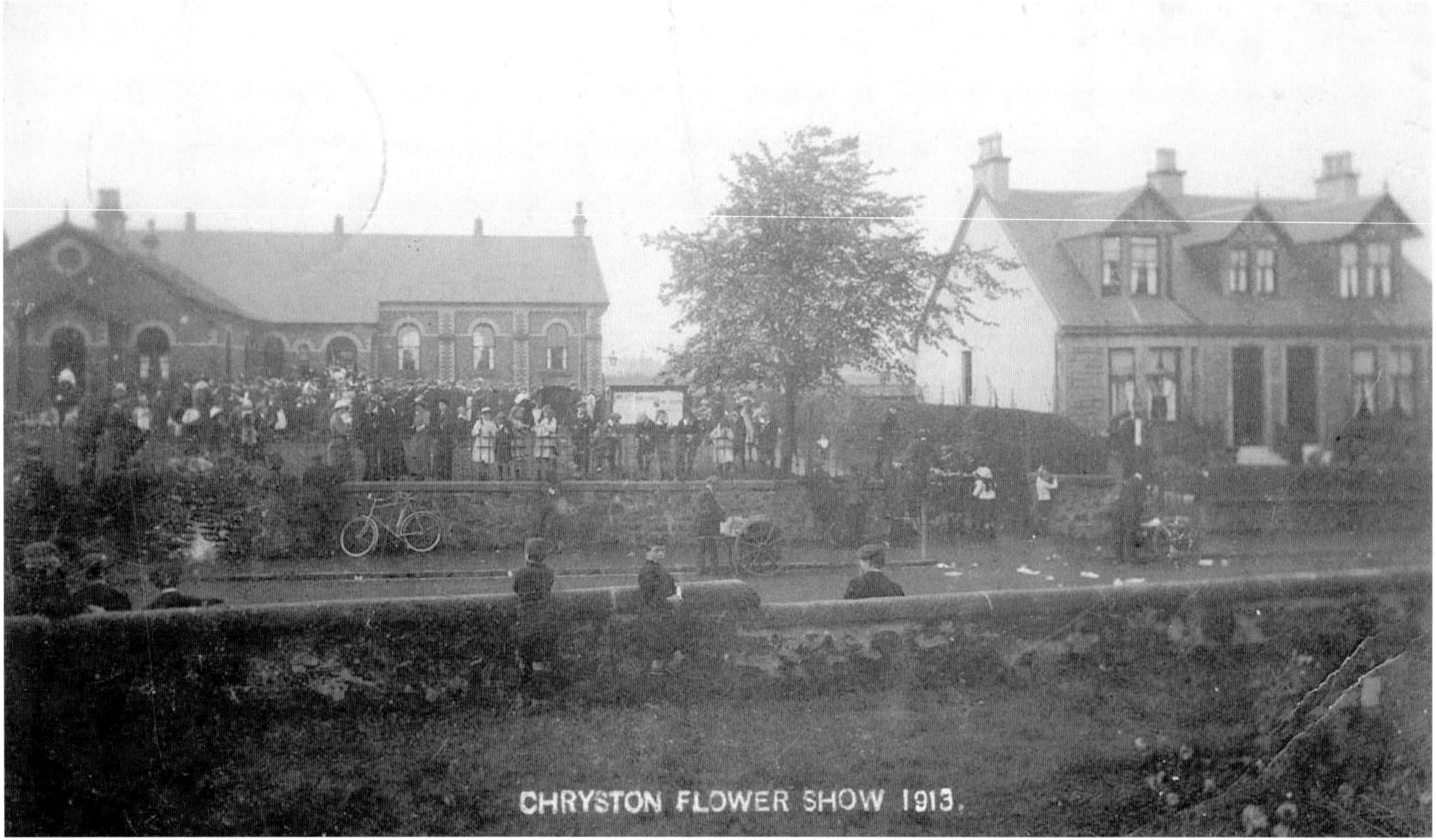

The 39th annual Chryston Flower Show, which opened on Saturday, 3 September 1913, was held – as had been the practice for a number of years – within Muirhead Public Hall. The show was organised by Chryston and District Horticultural Society, which was formed on 13 December 1853 and, initially, was composed of 'amateurs, gentlemen gardeners and others, whether cultivating for profit or otherwise'. Of the 733 entries in 1913, there were 208 entries within the 'gardeners' class, 256 within the 'amateurs' class, and 115 bouquets of wild flowers submitted by local school children! The event was hosted by Walter Cross Buchanan Christie, Honorary President of the society, with music performed on the green outside the hall by the Kirkintilloch Silver Band. The semi-detached villa to the right of the hall was built in the late 1890s and comprises the properties known as Woodstock and Corlig. During the first half of the twentieth century, these homes were occupied by members of the Walkinshaw family, who ran a local joinery business for many years.

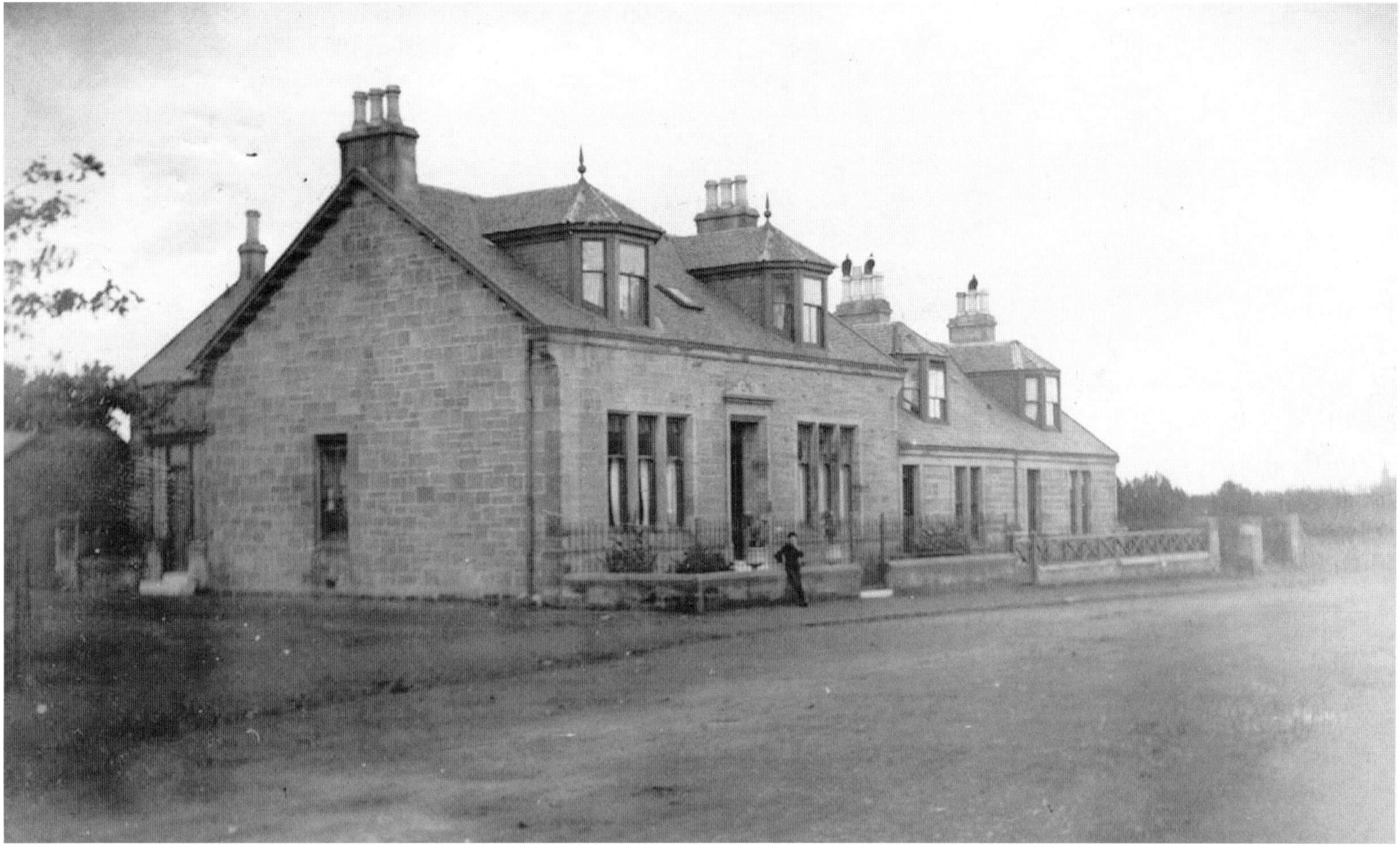

These two conjoined properties, seen here around 1906, are located on the north side of Cumbernauld Road, at the corner of Bowling Green Road. Although both externally remain largely unchanged, the near half of the house closest to the camera was later converted for use as a shop by replacing the three narrow windows with a single wider one. This shop was run by local butcher, Harry Marshall, and was one of five butcher shops in the village in the 1950s. Customers included the occupants of Bedlay House, who were regularly supplied with baskets of fresh meat by Harry's delivery boys, who cycled between the shop and the house. Later owners of the shop included Cathie and George Mitchell, and their son (also George), who, in addition to butcher meat, also sold fish. George sold the shop around 2004 and it is presently the Feast sandwich bar.

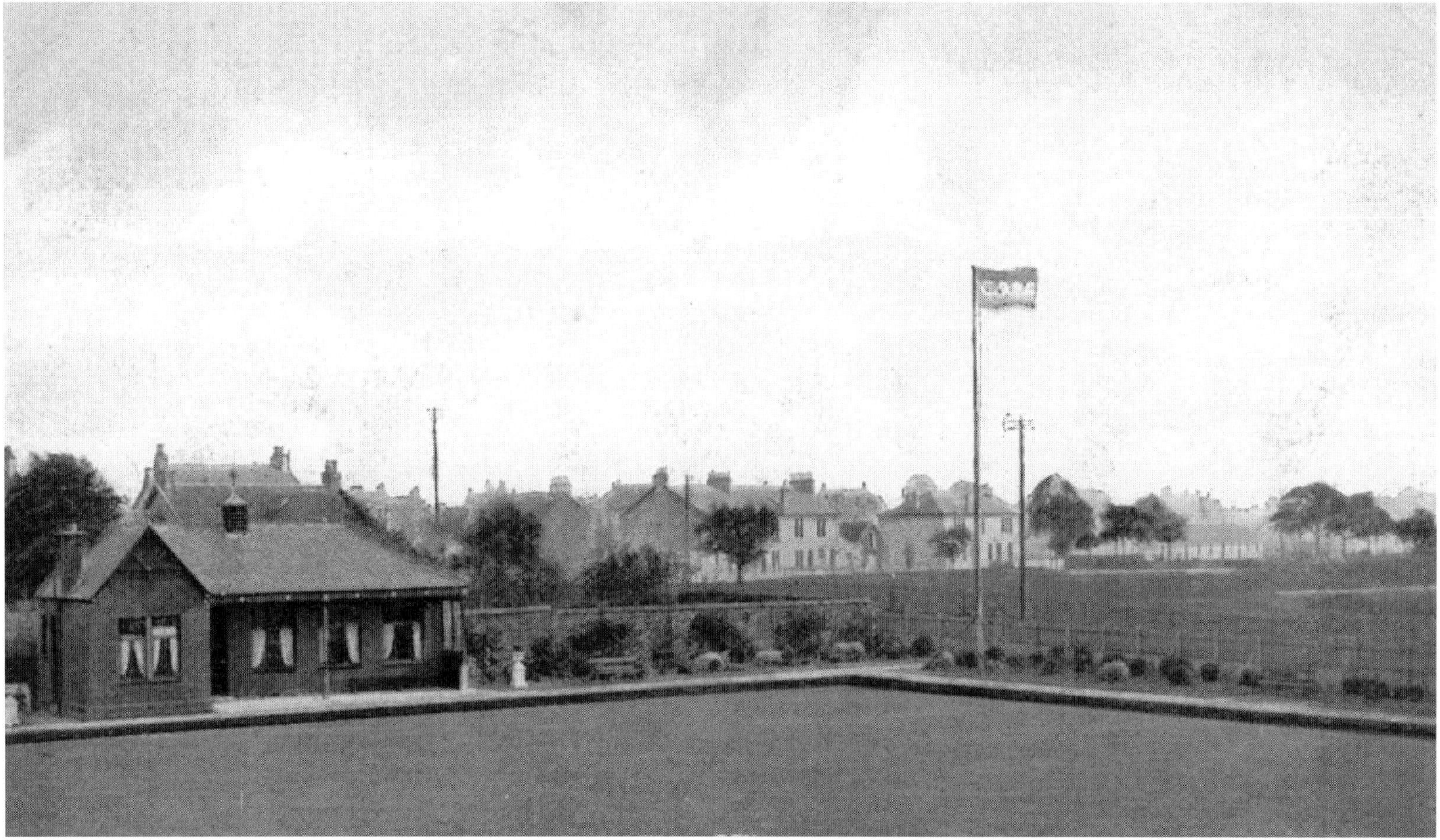

In this early view of Muirhead, part of the open 'muir' from which the village takes its name can be seen on the right, to the west of the Chryston Bowling Club green. As the hollow on the muir was often waterlogged, it was frequently used by cattle drovers taking their animals to the markets in Glasgow or Falkirk. Although this practice eventually diminished, as late as 1931 the Clerk to Cadder District Council was required to write requesting payment from a local farmer who was grazing his cows on the muir. However, payment was refused by the farmer on the basis that the muir was 'sorely trampled on' (perhaps by the cattle?!). Ultimately, an agreement was reached to allow the farmer free use of the muir for grazing, provided he cut the grass on a regular basis. As an extra incentive, he was allowed to retain the cut grass to feed his cattle. Ultimately, this arrangement ceased when the muir was laid out as a public park. Toilet facilities were added in 1956, on the site of an ex-ARP Decontamination Centre which had been erected during the Second World War.

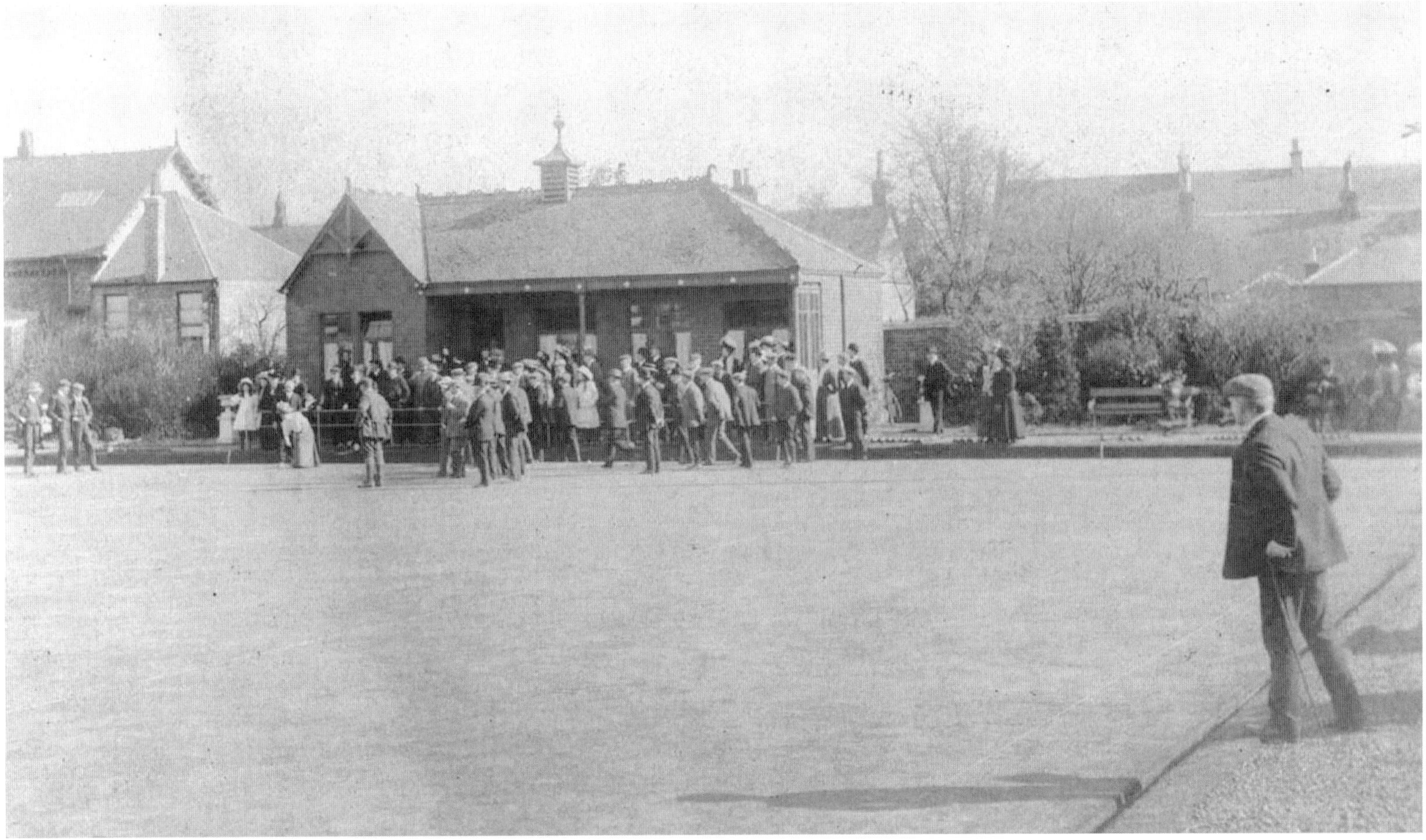

In this photograph from around 1910 members of Chryston Bowling Club and their families are gathered around the club president's wife as she prepares to throw the first jack, thus marking the annual opening of the green. Formed in 1900, the club can proudly boast that it was the first sporting club to be established in the district. Its clubhouse (or pavilion, as it was once called), which can be seen behind the assembled guests, was opened around 1904. Since then, the clubhouse has been altered and extended on several occasions, most notably in September 1992 when a further extension was opened by local MP, Tom Clarke. A second green was opened in 1947, alongside the original green, when the club acquired the tennis court site of the defunct Chryston Tennis Club. At the time this photograph was taken, the primary function of the ladies pictured would have been to prepare the refreshments, customarily served at the conclusion of play. However, by 1914, when membership was extended to ladies, they would also have been keen participants in the opening day's play.

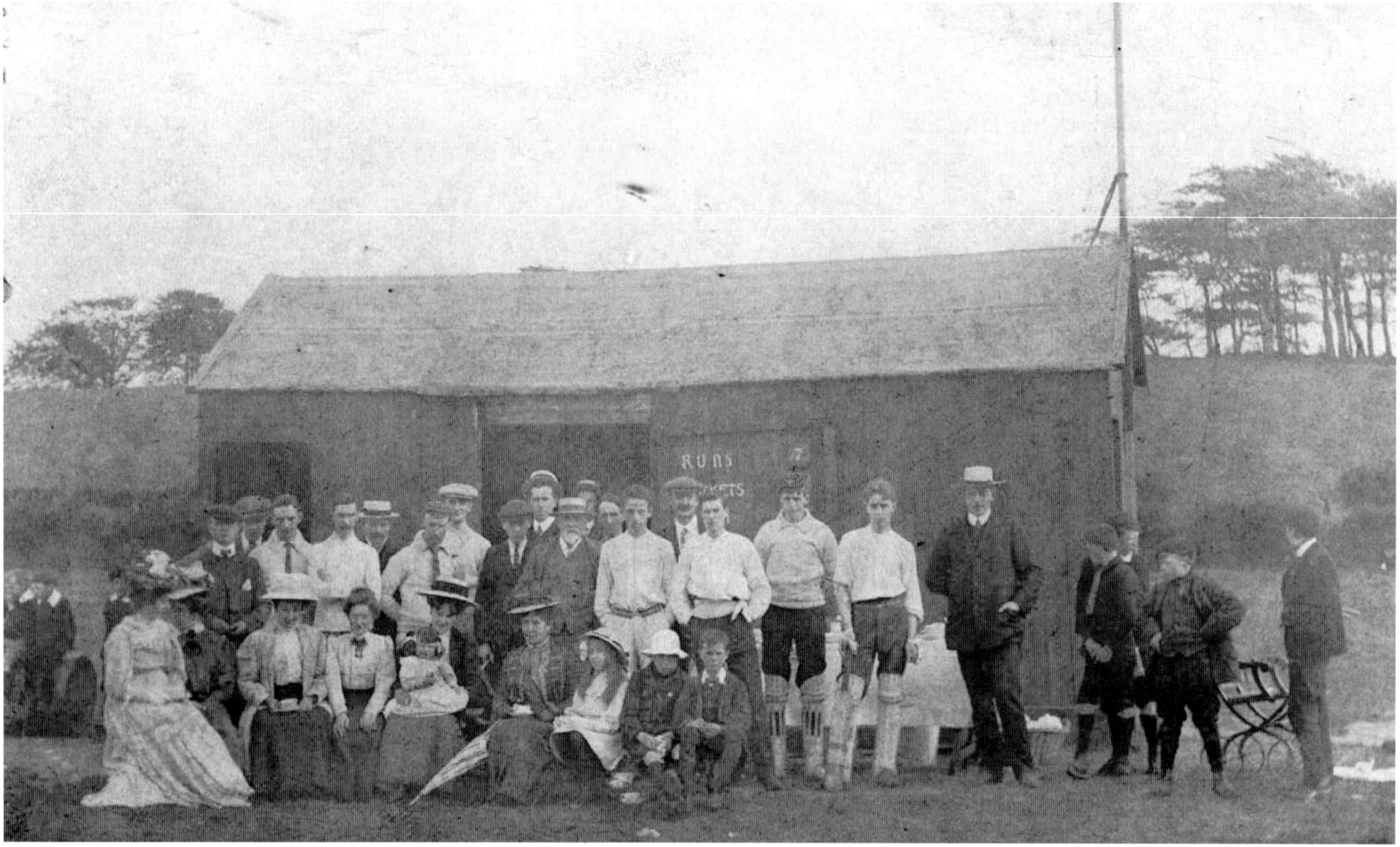

Following a meeting held in Muirhead Public Hall in late 1904, chaired by Charles D. Riggs, the then recently appointed Chairman of Cadder Parish Council, it was agreed to found a cricket club, to be known as the Chryston and District Cricket Club. At this meeting, which despite inclement weather had attracted thirty prospective members, it was also agreed to accept the offer by James Jackson, the farmer at Chryston Mains, to let land previously used as a football ground for use by the club. Although their first season got off to a bad start, with a reported 'dusting', the new club quickly recovered, posting successive wins against teams of the calibre of Lumloch, Victoria Park, Springfield and the 28th Glasgow Boys' Brigade. Despite this, within a few years Chryston and District Cricket Club appears to have been disbanded.

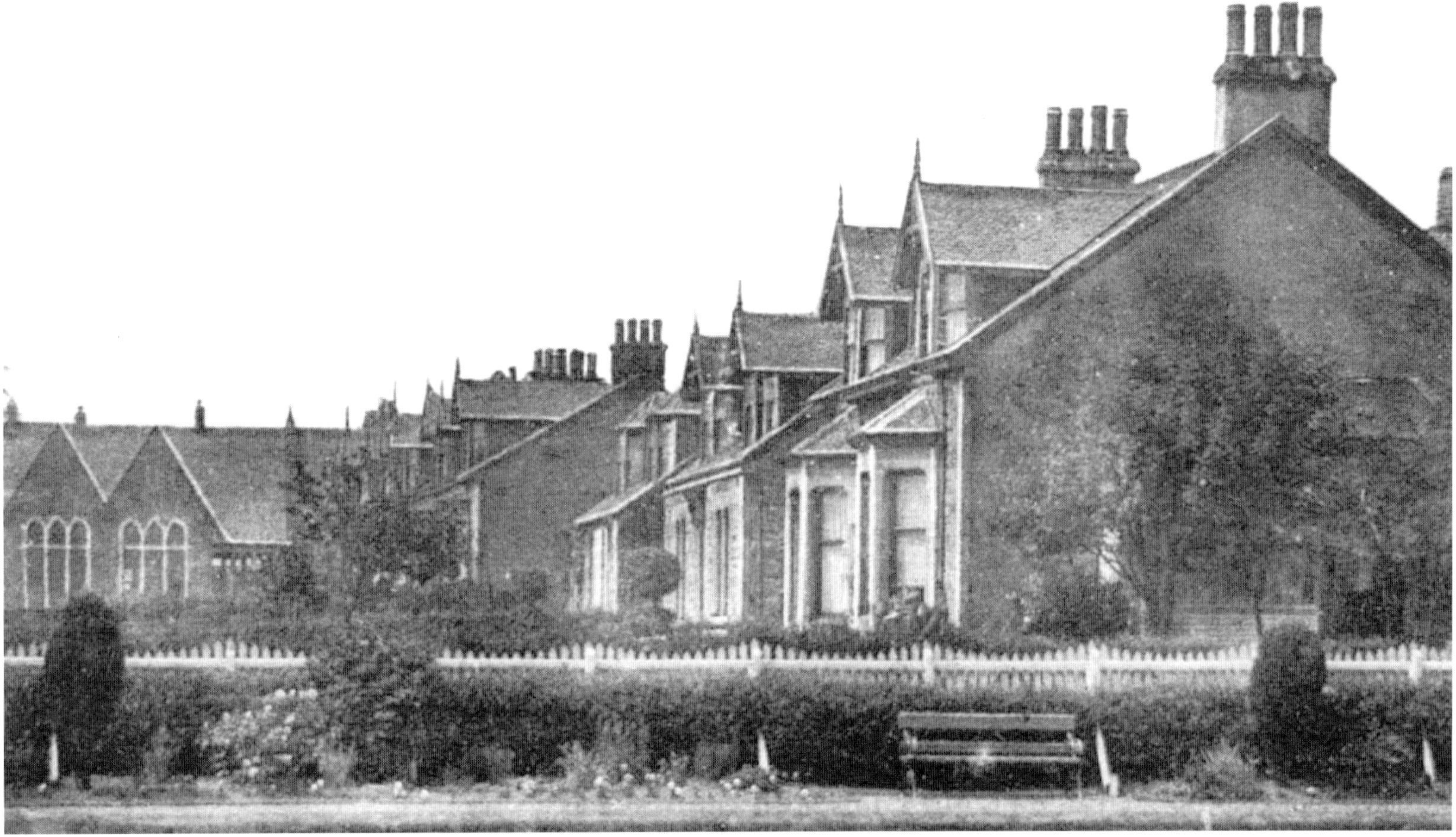

This view, taken from the Chryston Bowling Club's green, shows the villas on Park Road. These were built in the late 1800s and include Parkview, which at one time was the home of David Jackson, a prominent local citizen. To the left, facing the camera, is the eastern gable of Chryston Public School. The foundation stone of this school was laid on 26 June 1875 by Thomas Craig Christie of Bedlay House and the school opened in 1877. It was built under the auspices of the Cadder School Board and replaced three village schools – the old parish school, the Free Church school and a local school for girls. When first built, the public school comprised nine classrooms and one staffroom, with a separate house for the headmaster. On various occasions over the years the school was extended, however, in December 1975, following the erection of new school buildings, it was demolished. The site was subsequently cleared for the erection of the present-day Chilterns Home for the Elderly, which was opened on 21 April 1978.

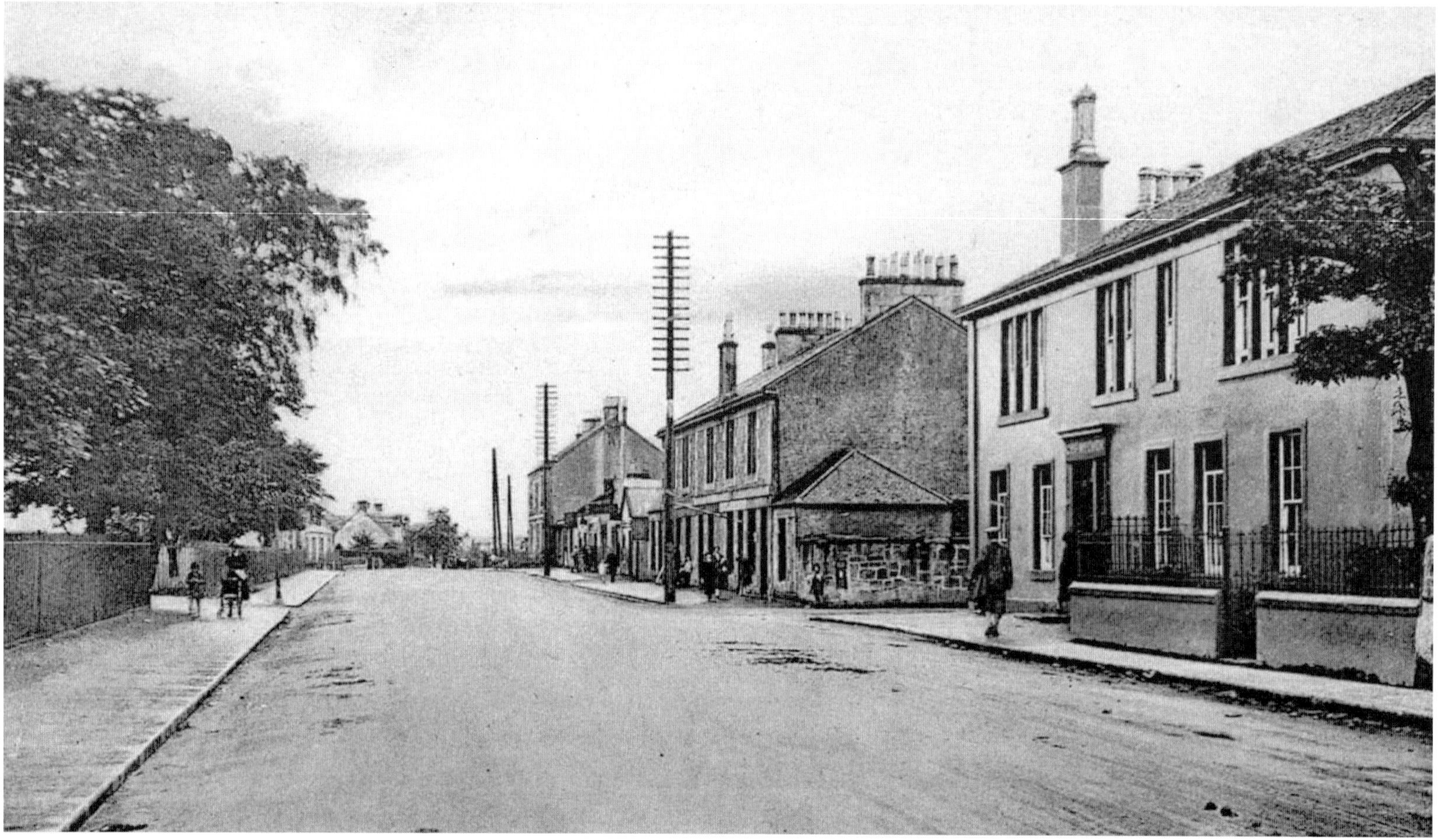

This early view of Muirhead, looking east, features some of the older buildings on the south side of Cumbernauld Road. These include, at the corner of Station Road, the long-established Muirhead Inn. Although there were a large number of licensed premises in and around Muirhead before the turn of the twentieth century, the local 'baton-men' who policed the area were said to have 'little to do' as regards drunk and disorderly behaviour. Despite this, J.C. Robertson, an ardent Salvationist from Denny, was so concerned about the amount of drink consumed in Chryston and Muirhead, that during 1909 he paid several visits to the district. Rejoicing in the name of 'the pub smasher', Robertson claimed he came 'not wielding an axe but a bible'. It is reported that on one visit, he went into Muirhead Inn to persuade customers not to drink away their hard-earned cash and, later that evening, held a public meeting outside the gates of the public park (which can be seen to the left of photograph).

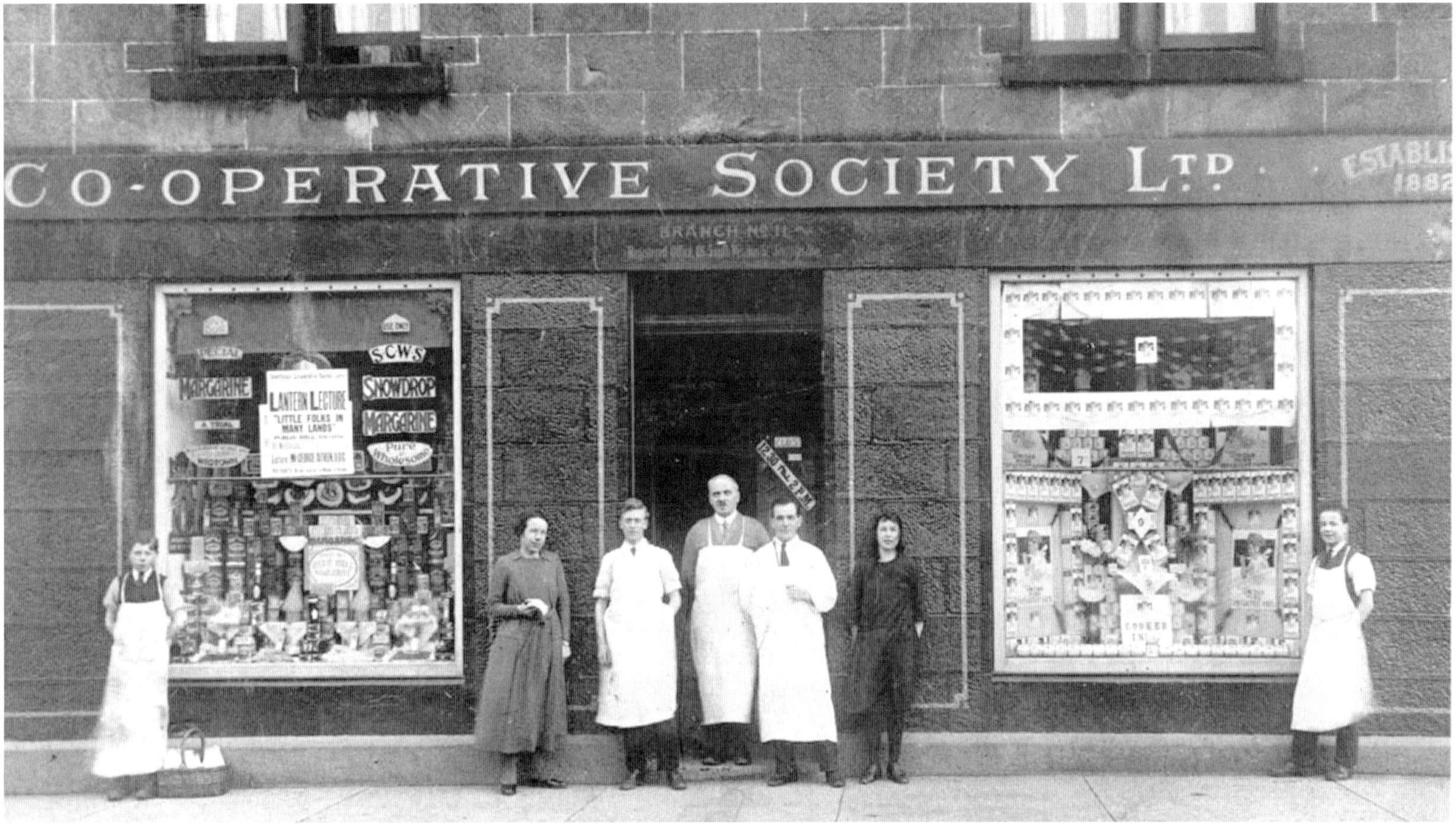

In this photograph from the mid 1920s, the staff of Shettleston Co-operative Society's No. 11 grocery branch are assembled outside their store in Station Road, Muirhead. From around 1892 until 1919, when an amalgamation scheme was agreed, these premises had been operated by the smaller independent Chryston District Co-operative Society. This society, in addition to their Station Road store, also had a horse and cart, which was used to deliver individual wicker baskets of goods to customers in outlying areas. Although the endeavours of the smaller society had reportedly met with some degree of success, the imposition of wartime rationing prompted the management to amalgamate with the larger Shettleston Society. Once amalgamation was assured, the Station Road branch was completely reorganised and, shortly afterwards, a butchery department was opened alongside. Later still, a drapery branch (just out of photograph, on the left) was opened. In the early 1920s, a second co-operative society, the Coatbridge Co-operative Society, opened a suite of shops on Cumbernauld Road, so that for much of the twentieth century Muirhead was served by not one, but two, co-operative societies.

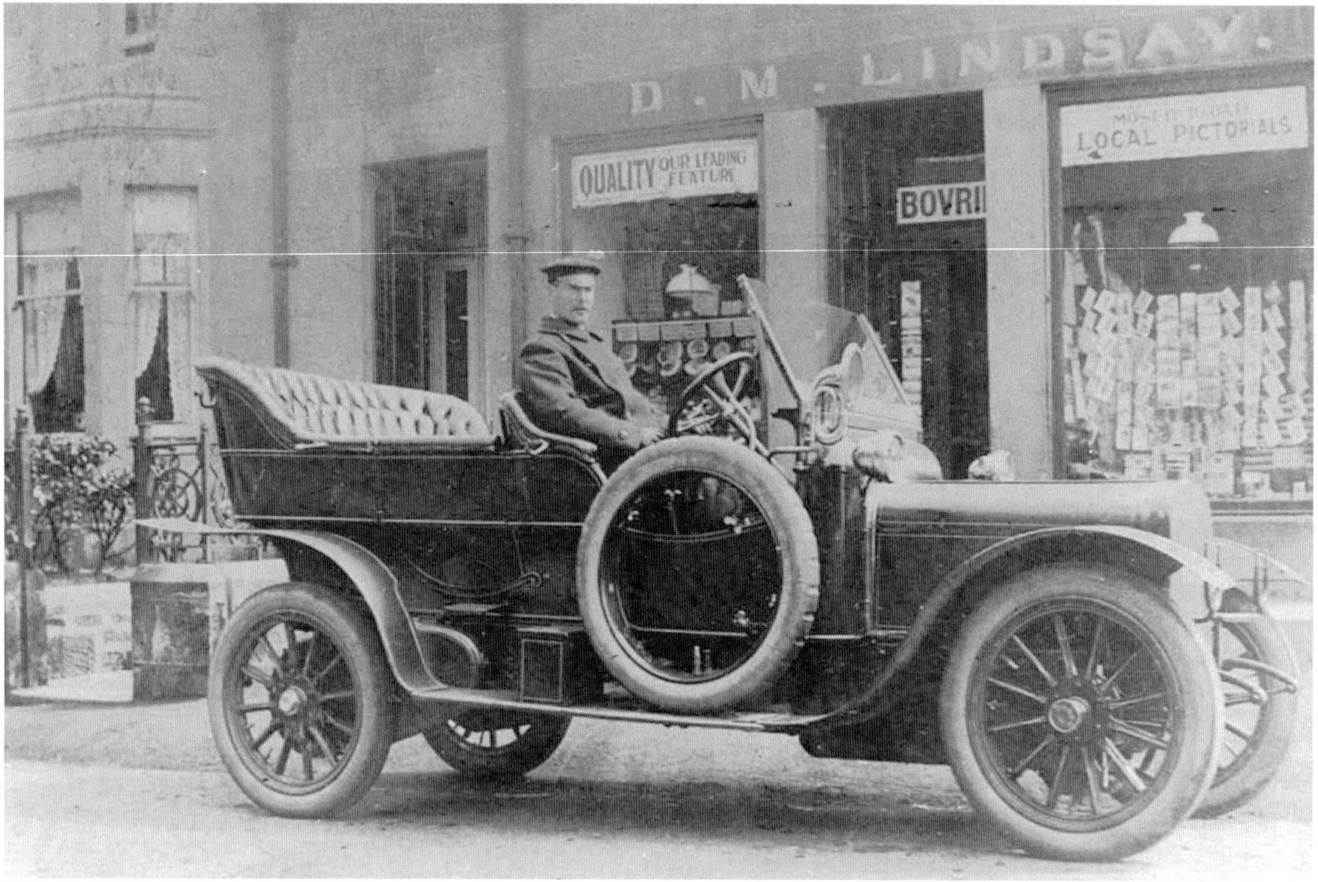

The post office and grocery shop, which was situated on Station Road, at the corner of Elmira Road, was one of the most frequented shops in Muirhead. Around the turn of the last century, it was run by George Craig Murphy. Murphy, who had another grocery shop and post office in nearby Glenboig, was an active member of Chryston Bowling Club and a very well-respected figure in the district. Around 1921, the business was taken over by Duncan Lindsay. Lindsay was a keen photographer and, as can be seen from the 'local pictorials' sign in the right-hand window, he obviously combined his hobby with his business. Like Murphy, Lindsay was also an active member of Chryston Bowling Club and, during the Second World War, was active in raising funds for the Chryston District Welcome Home Fund. After Lindsay's retirement, the shop and post office was run by his son, Tom, and later by Irvine McNish. In 1999, the post office was closed when a new purpose-built post office was opened within the new Co-operative Building, further along Cumbernauld Road. The official opening of the new post office was carried out by local MP, Tom Clarke, and Mrs Violet Campbell, a 90-year-old Muirhead resident. The former post office and grocery shop is presently occupied by hairdresser Karen Bryce.

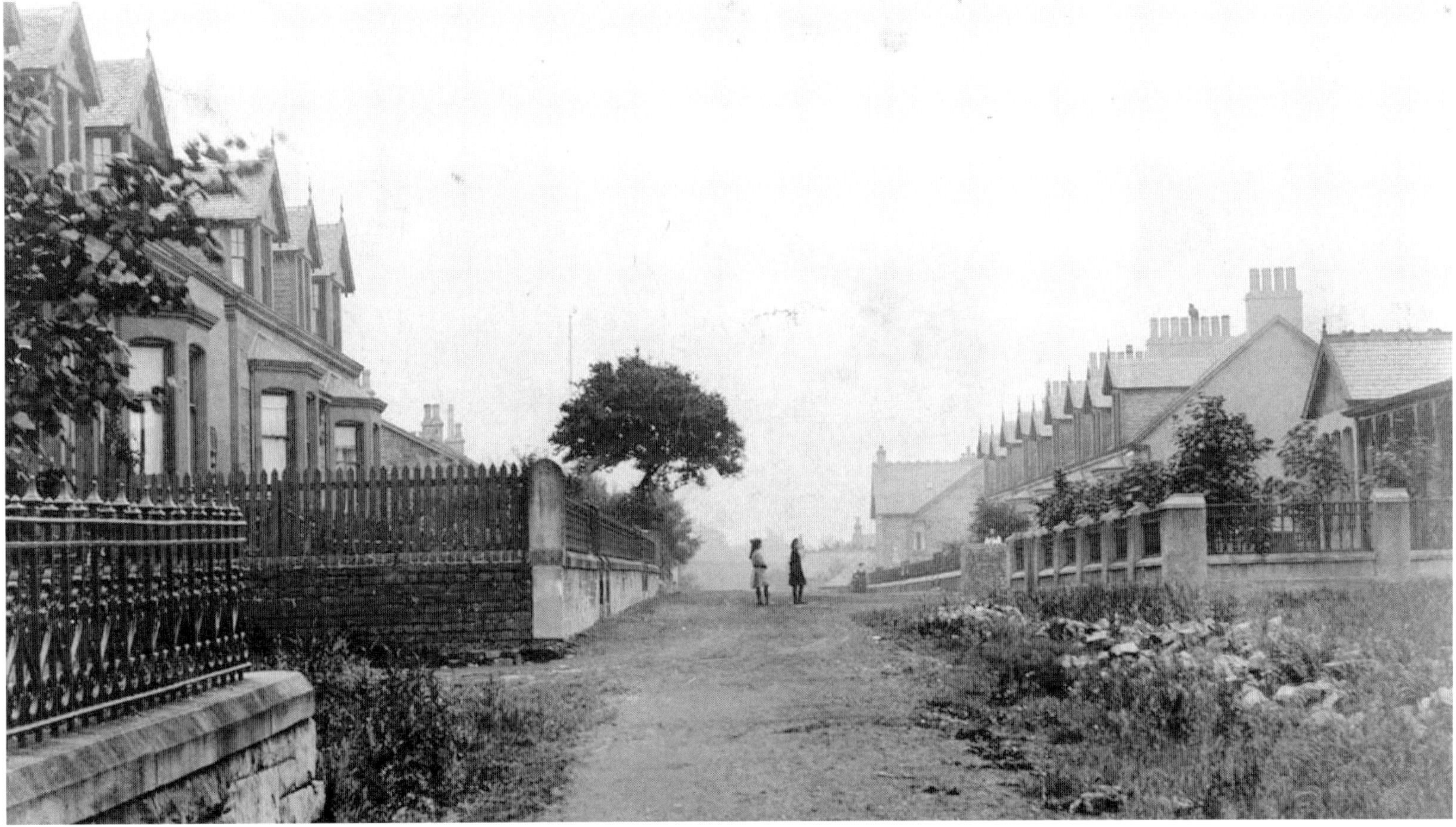

By 1910, when this postcard was sent, the earlier development of terraced houses (seen here to right of photograph, all with matching roof dormers) had been joined by similarly styled houses on the opposite side of Potassels Road. The former were built around 1901 by the Distillers Company for middle management, on land possibly formerly owned by nearby Potassels Farm. Indeed, the bungalow named Sefton, on the extreme right of photograph, is said to have been built on the site of the farm's duck pond. Beyond these villas, at the entrance to Potassels Road, is Esslemont, then the home of Dr Lamont. On left of photograph, occupying one half of the first semi-detached villa, is Rydal Mount. For a period this was occupied by George Jackson, who had previously farmed at Woodhead Farm. In 1913, a relative, James Jackson, then farming at Berryknowe, organised a 'get together' on behalf of the entire Jackson family to mark the centenary of the family's presence on the Garnkirk Estate. Amongst the invited guests was John Wotherspoon, who farmed here at West Potassels.

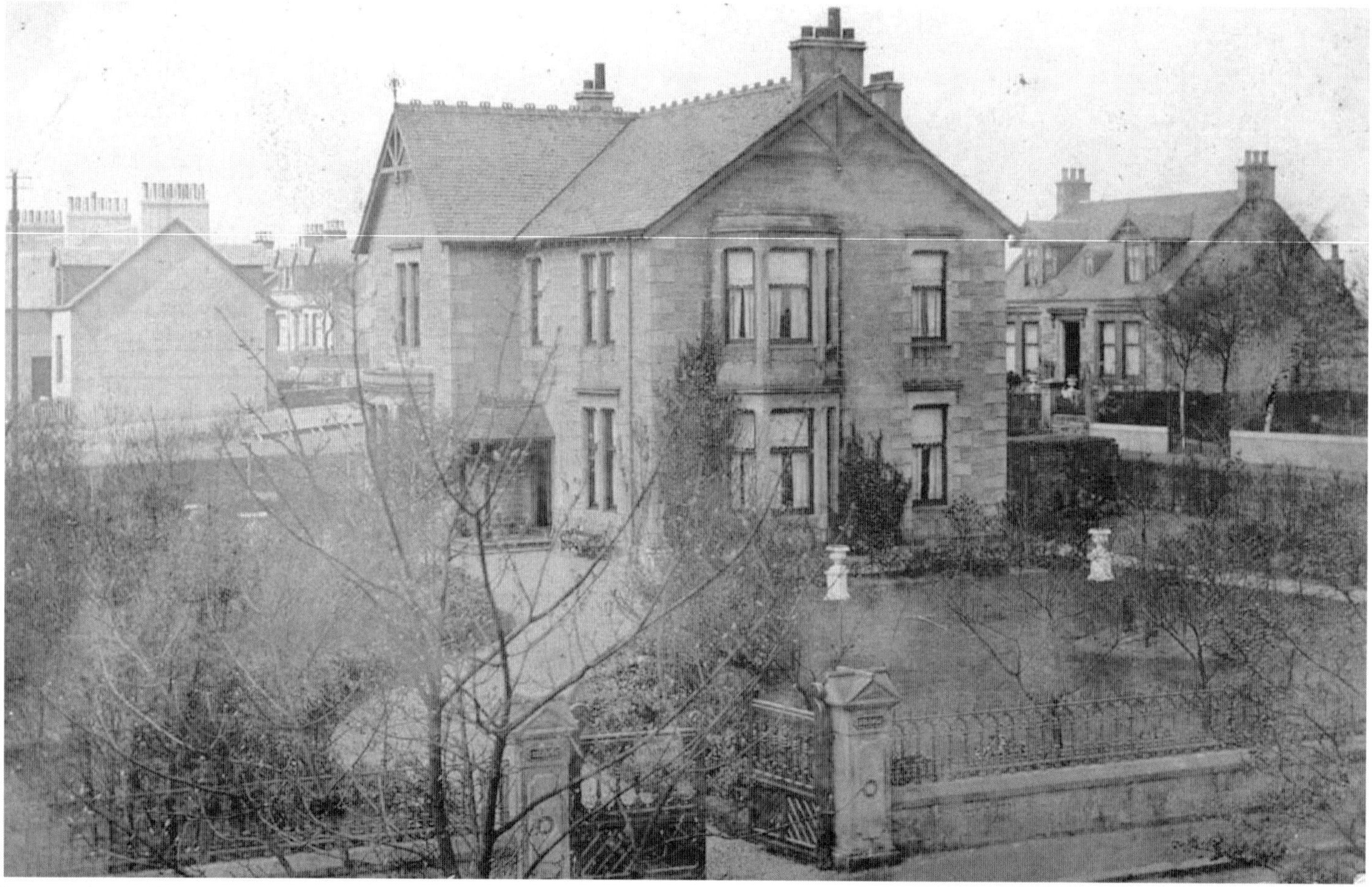

From about 1892, until his retiral in 1920, Esslemont was the residence of well-respected local doctor, Alexander Lamont. No doubt over the years Dr Lamont would have had many unexpected visitors, but perhaps none more unexpected than Gustav Hamel, an early aviation pioneer, who almost literally 'dropped in for tea'! While competing in the prestigious Daily Mail Air Race on 26 July 1911, Hamel was forced to make an unscheduled landing nearby, when his Bleriot monoplane developed a fault. Hamel was then invited to tea with the doctor while repairs were being carried out to his plane. Dr Lamont was later succeeded by the equally respected Dr Andrew Maguire, who resided in Esslemont until his death in 1950. Surrounding Esslemont in this photograph are some of the properties on Potassels Road, including, on the extreme right of photograph, Ardenvohr, home of the Jackson family until 1955. The decorative plant holders in the gardens of both Esslemont and Ardenvohr, which were made by the local fireclay works, have now become collectors' items.

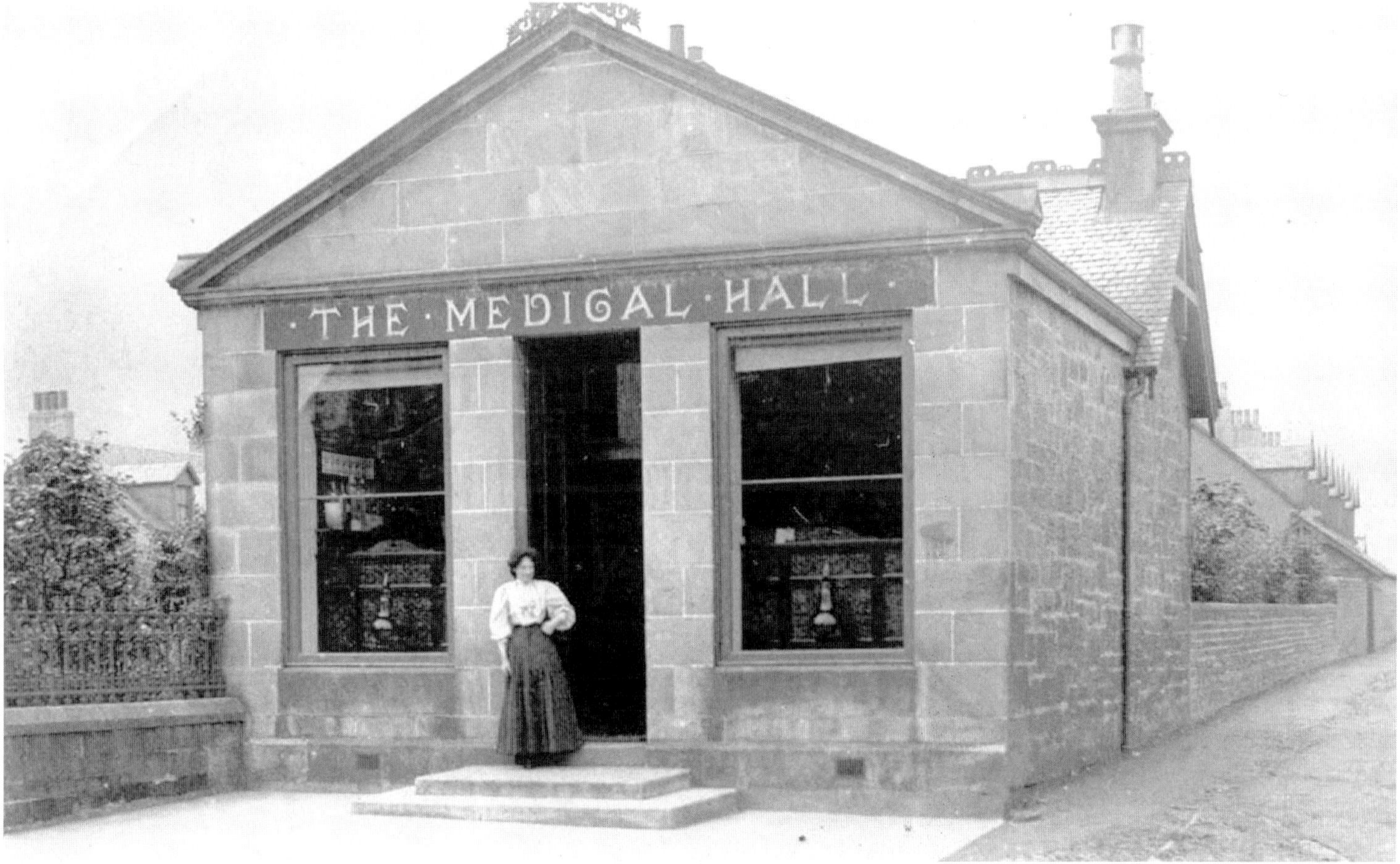

During the times of Doctors Lamont and Maguire, the single-storey Medical Hall (seen here to the front of Esslemont, at the corner of Station Road and Potassels Road) was utilised as a surgery. At one time, medical halls were a common feature of doctors' practices, thus enabling doctors, as far as possible, to keep their private life separate from their medical activities. The tall containers in the front windows indicate that this particular hall was also used for the preparation and dispensing of medicines. Although the hall continued to be used as a surgery until well into the 1950s, the dispensing of medicines ceased in 1922, when Thomas McLean opened the village's first chemist shop, in Oakbank on Cumbernauld Road. When the doctor's practice was relocated to Stepps, the hall lay empty for a number of years, before being let out to a succession of short-term owners. Presently it is occupied by Blitz Group Limited, who service ventilation systems and undertake industrial cleaning services. Today the hall, externally at least, is largely unchanged in appearance. The roof ornamentation on both the hall and Esslemont are further examples of the output of the local fireclay works.

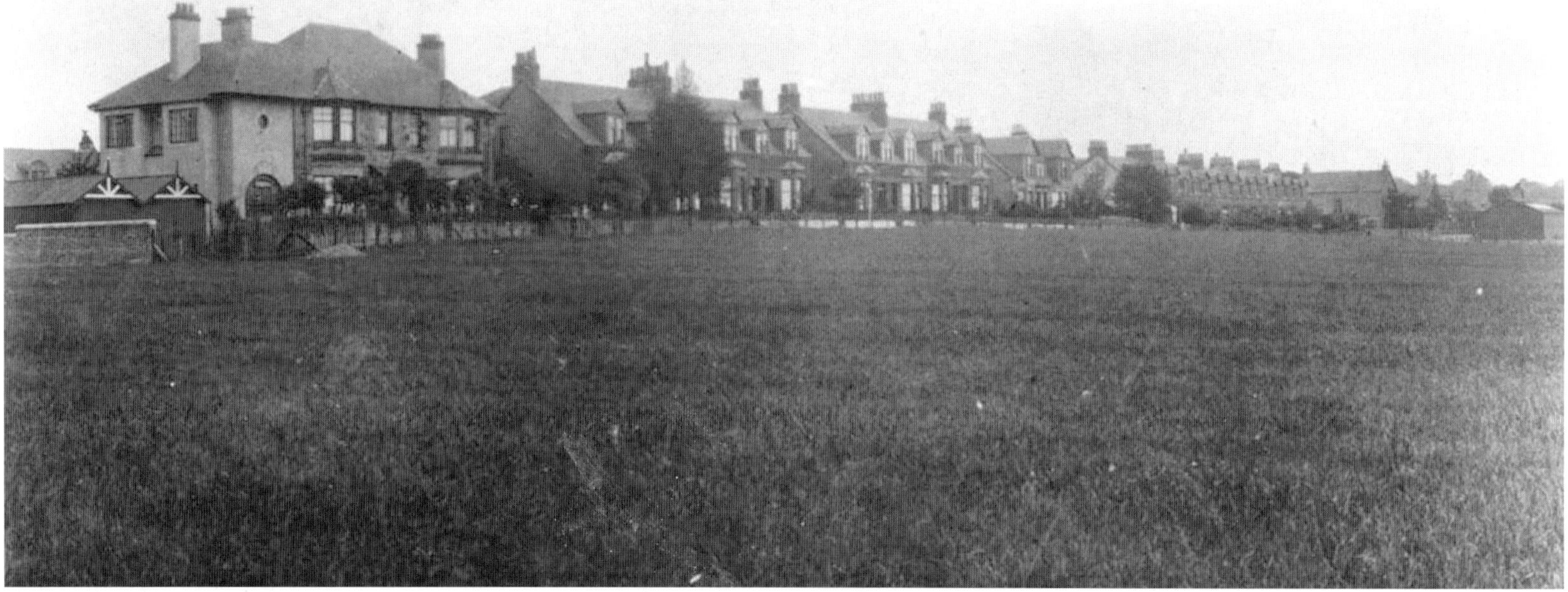

This photograph shows the matching blocks of terraced houses, complete with roof dormers, originally known as Lilybank Terrace and situated on present-day Lilybank Avenue. These houses were erected around 1904, next to fields belonging to Woodhead Farm. In such a position, the original occupants of these homes would most probably have had panoramic views of the surrounding countryside, in addition to benefiting from their close proximity to Garnkirk Station. Alongside the terraced housing, to the extreme left of the photograph, is Abergeldie. In recent years, this was the home of local businessman, Cyril Clark, whose Spar supermarket was opened on Cumbernauld Road in February 1979. To the right of the terraced housing can be seen the house known as Tantallon, with its garage being to extreme right of photograph. For many years this property was the residence of William James Fleming, a senior partner in Fleming Brothers, a Glasgow-based structural engineering firm. A well-respected businessman, Fleming, who died in 1947, is buried in nearby Bedlay Cemetery. Today, the majority of the houses seen here have survived, and new houses have been built in the field opposite the older properties.

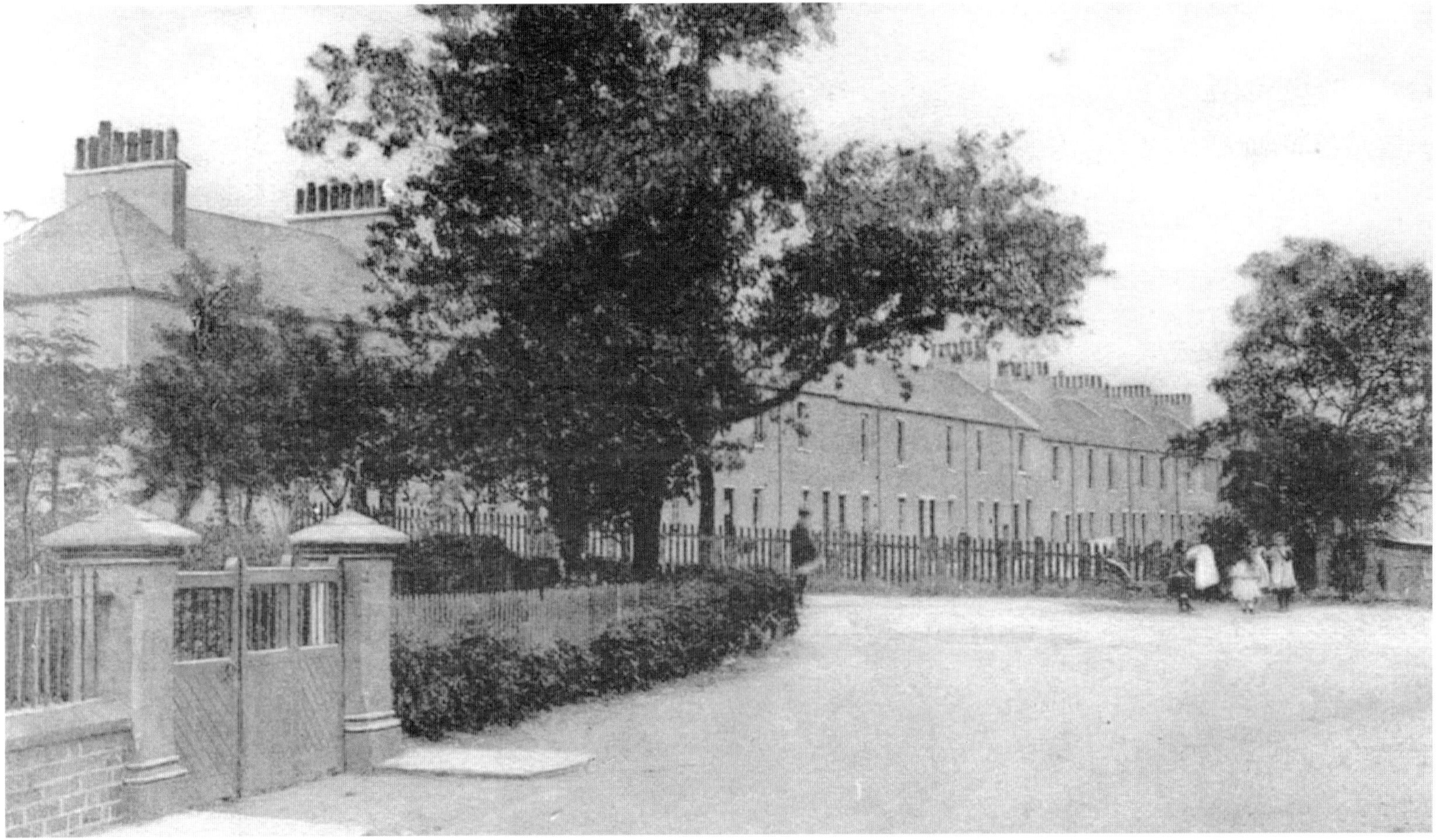

In this early photograph, taken from the entrance to Neuk Avenue, can be seen the back greens of the terraced two-storey houses built around the turn of the twentieth century on the south side of Drumcavel Road at Mossvale. This housing comprised two blocks, known as Alexandra Parade and Edward Place, and was owned by coal masters James Nimmo & Company. Their occupants, for the most part, were miners, ironmongers, bricklayers and labourers, employed in either the local colliery or fireclay works. On nationalisation of the coal industry in 1948, the houses became the property of the National Coal Board, and remained so until their demolition in the late 1950s. In contrast to this terraced housing, a substantial property comprising two semi-detached homes was also built in Neuk Avenue at the same time, purportedly for senior officials employed in one of the local fireclay works. These homes are known as Bellfield and Annfield, and the gate to the latter can be seen to extreme left of photograph.

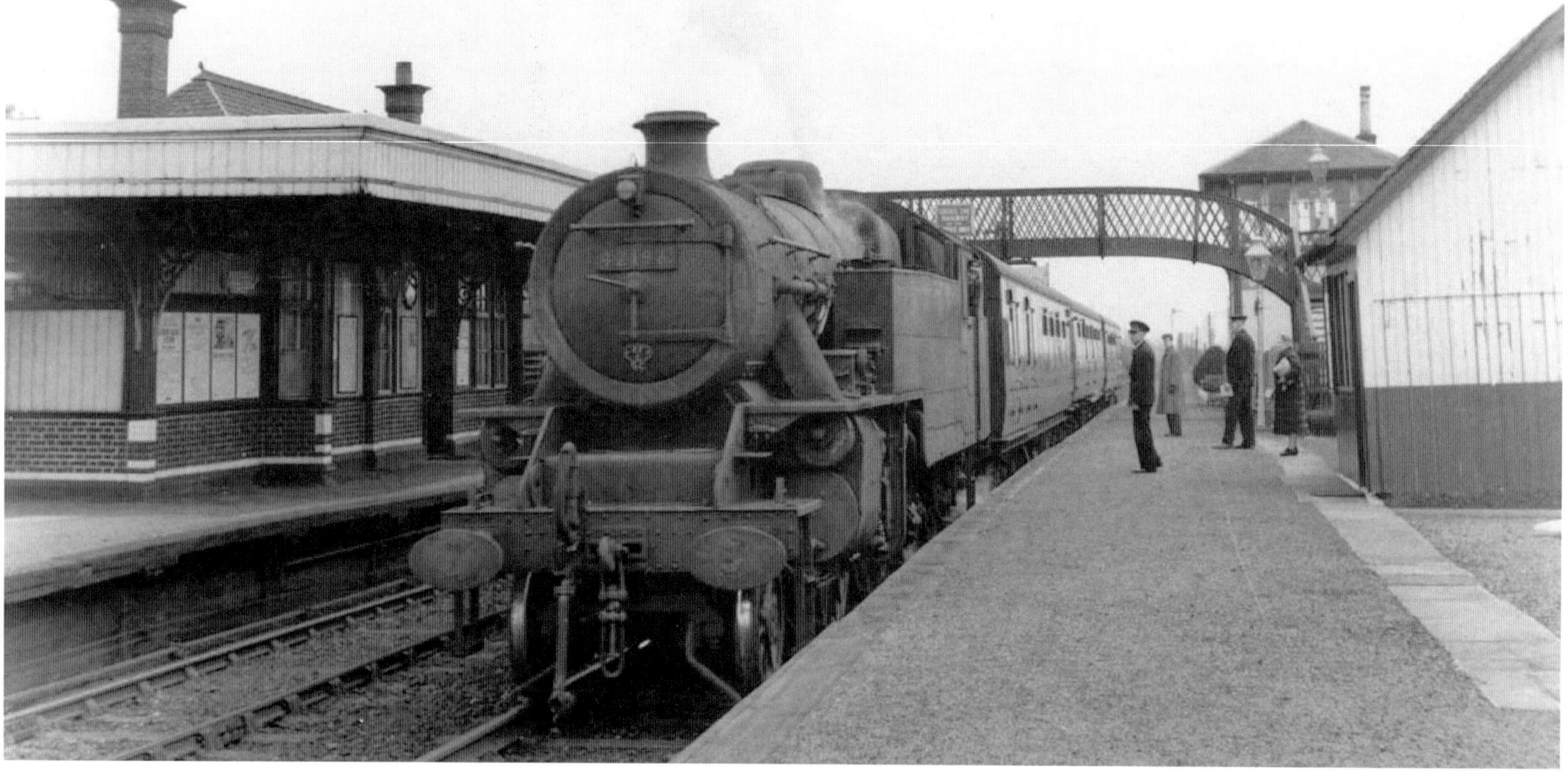

Garnkirk Station, seen here in March 1960, shortly before closure, was one of several intermediate stations on the former Garnkirk & Glasgow Railway. One of the earliest public railways in Scotland, it was opened principally to convey coal from the Monklands coalfield to Glasgow. The traditional 'breaking of ground' ceremony, to signal the start of construction, was carried out on 28 August 1827 by Mrs Harriet Sprot of Garnkirk, and the line was officially opened on 27 September 1831. Although initially Garnkirk Station had no booking office, waiting rooms or raised platforms, these were later added as passenger traffic increased. Despite its remoteness from the surrounding villages, the line was well used until about 1914, when it began to suffer from competition from the bus companies. This mainly came from local bus operator, Rankin Brothers, one of the most successful of the early bus pioneers. Founded by Thomas L. Rankin (or 'TL' as he was better known), his brothers Will and Bob, and local man Johnnie Madden, by the time the business was sold to William Alexander & Sons in 1929 it had become the largest privately owned bus operator in Scotland. The engine seen here in this photograph from 4 March 1960 is 2-6-4T No. 42196 with the 1.37 p.m. service from Gartcosh to Glasgow Buchanan Street.

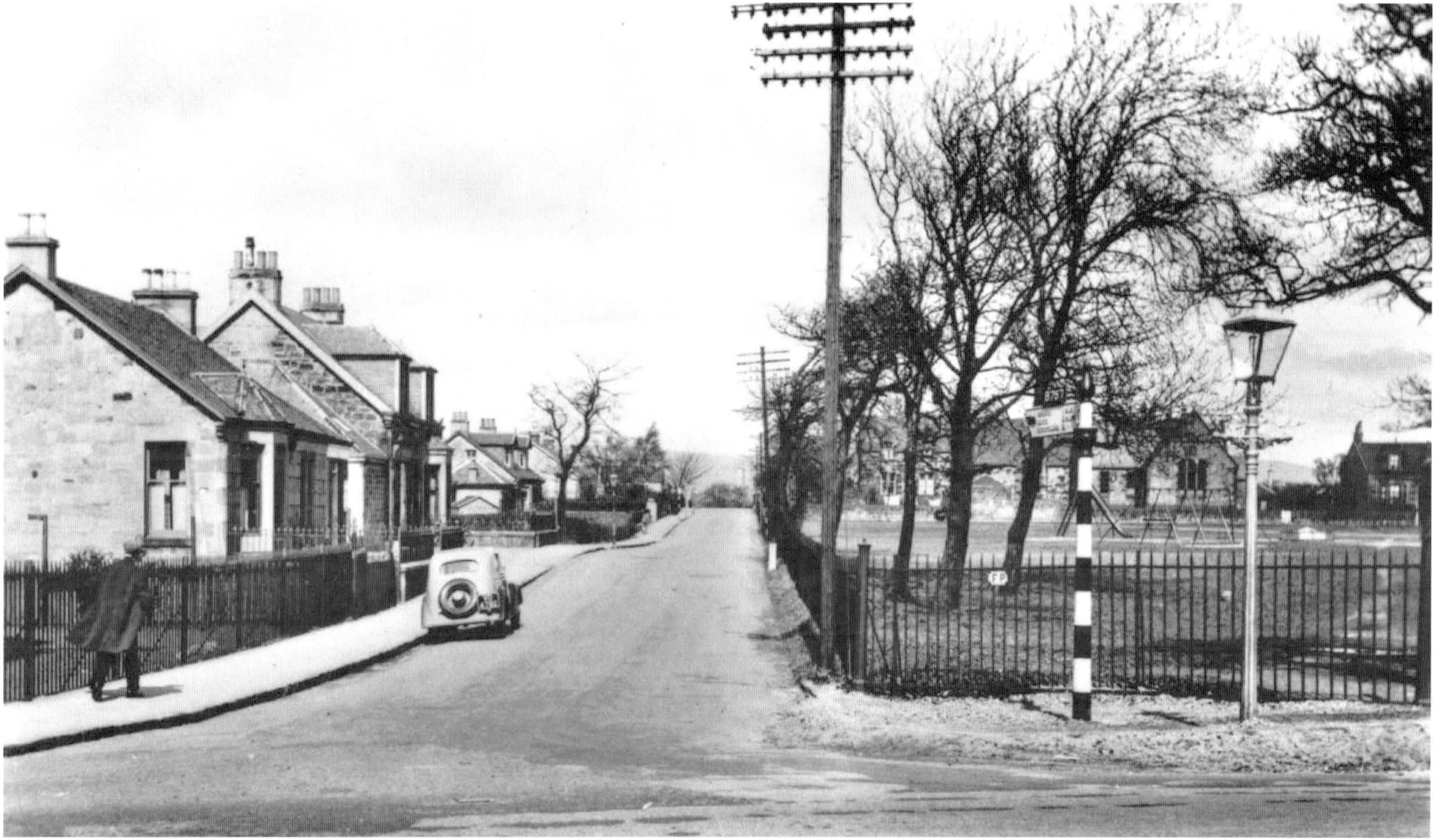

Of the houses seen here on the west side of Lindsaybeg Road in this 1930s photograph, the two nearest the camera have both served as shops. The first property (with the Model C Ford parked beside it) is Alexandra Villa which, in the early years of the twentieth century, was owned by Robert Jack, who utilised part of the property as a dairy. Although the official name for the business was Townhead Dairy, locally it was generally referred to as 'Jack's Dairy'. Subsequent owners of the property included John Harvey (who operated a drapery and 'jenny-a'-things') and, around 1950, Tom Hailstone, whose Muirhead Electrical Services was located here. The second property in the photograph, which is distinguishable by its two roof dormers, is Crossford (presently known as Viewpark). In the 1920s this was owned by John McPherson, whose butcher shop occupied part of the building. Later owners (and all butchers) included Nessie Letham, Willie McFarlane, John Perkins, Tom Moffat and, since around 1979, the very popular Stewart Collins & Son.

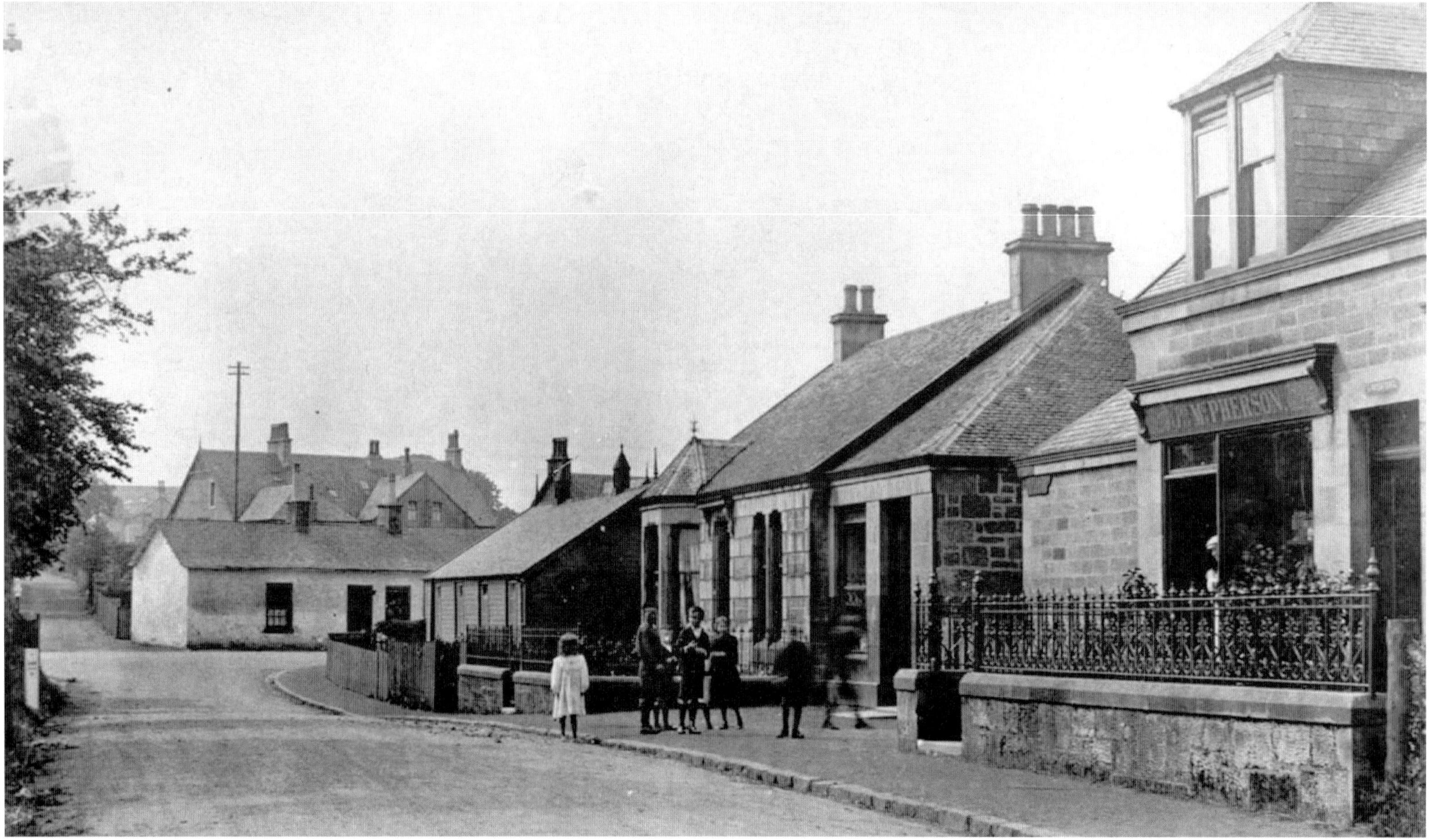

In this view, looking south towards Cumbernauld Road, we can clearly see Crossford (with John McPherson's butcher shop) and Alexandra Villa (with Robert Jack's Townhead Dairy). Beyond them, at the corner of Lindsaybeg Road, is the old Muirhead Evangelistic Hall. Known locally as the 'tin hall', it was built in the 1890s and was jointly run for almost fifty years by founder members John Pirie (a well-known west of Scotland tailor and draper) and William James Fleming, a senior partner in the Glasgow-based structural engineering firm of Fleming Brothers. The many years of service each gave is commemorated in plaques mounted in the vestibule of the present brick-built Moorpark Gospel Hall, which was opened in October 1957 on the site of the old hall. Beyond the hall, on the opposite side of Cumbernauld Road, is the former tollhouse, which was built around 1780 on the new turnpike road. Since the abolition of tolls in the late 1870s, the tollhouse has mostly been in private hands, except for a brief period when a branch of the Royal Bank of Scotland was housed here.

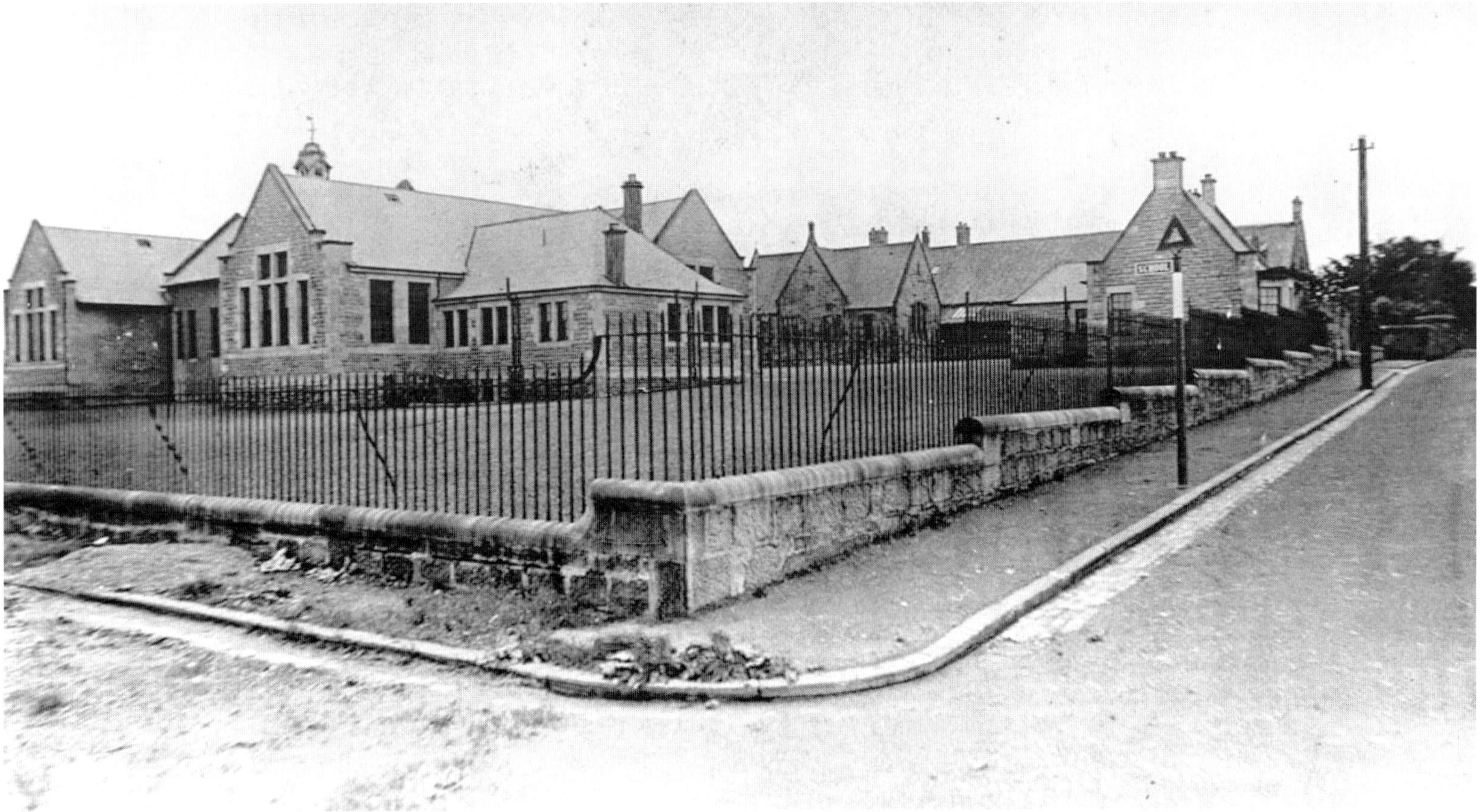

In 1908 a separate annexe for higher grade pupils (those aged 12 to 15 years old) was opened to the north of the old Chryston Public School. This annexe, in the foreground, to the left of the picture, was known locally as the 'new school'. It comprised a headmaster's room, seven classrooms and an assembly hall-cum-gymnasium. Any pupil wishing to stay on beyond school leaving age had then to travel to Coatbridge or Glasgow – a situation which incurred the wrath of the *Daily Mail* columnist 'The Judge', who in 1939 criticised Lanarkshire Education Authority for (as he saw it) putting brighter pupils at a considerable disadvantage. It was not until 1972 that this matter was partially rectified when the then newly named Chryston High School began taking pupils up to fourth year. In the 1960s both a new primary school and high school were built on a greenfield site to the rear of the higher grade annexe. The official opening of both schools on 6 March 1967 was undertaken by local councillor, Charles Gray. However, it was not until 1976, when Chryston High School was extended, that pupils could then continue their education locally up to sixth year. In 1988 the old higher grade annexe was badly damaged by fire and subsequently demolished.

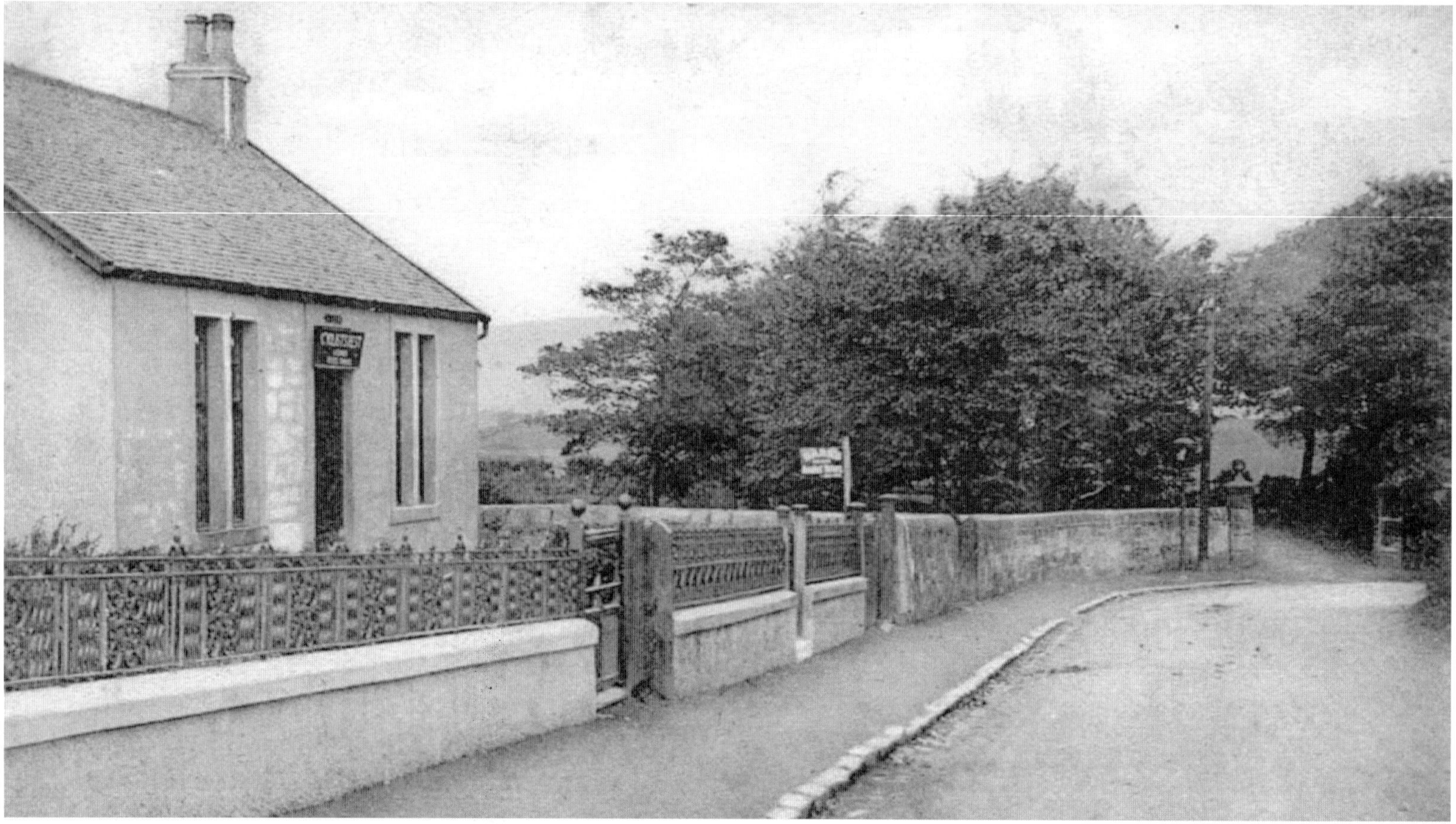

The now demolished Luton Cottage, seen here on Lindsaybeg Road around 1918, was built in the late 1870s for Jean Fyfe, the mother of James Fyfe, a celebrated local poet. During her occupancy of the cottage, a separate building to the rear of the cottage was used for her laundry business. Later, and at the time this photograph was taken, the cottage was a well-known 'cyclists' rest', where biscuits and soft drinks (in particular, Barr's Irn Bru, as the sign suggests) could be bought. Later occupants of the cottage included the Prouds, whose son Harry founded Chryston Pipe Band in 1920. In January 1939 Harry (who was the band's pipe major) and all but one of the band marched into the Glasgow headquarters of the newly formed 57th Searchlight Regiment Royal Artillery to join up, thereby ensuring that the regiment would have a ready-made pipe band of its own. To the right of Luton Cottage is the area known locally as the 'magazine', where material used for repairing local roads was kept by the council. Beyond this are the pillars of the Jubilee Gates, which gave access to Garnkirk House and Berryknowe Farm.

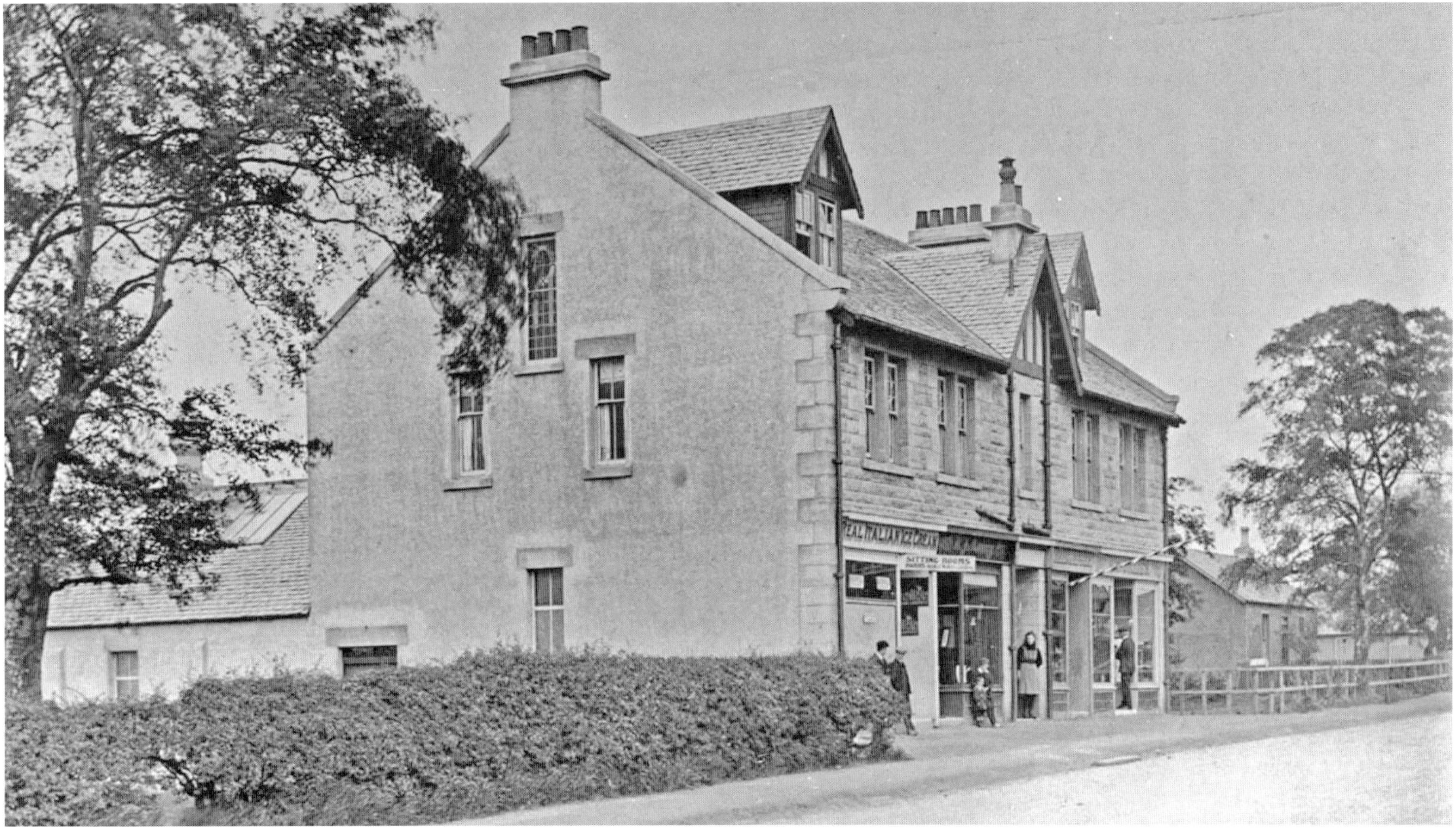

In this view, taken around 1915, can be seen the two-storey grey sandstone tenement on Cumbernauld Road, Muirhead, known variously as Oakbank Buildings, and Oakbank Terrace. At that time the ground floor shops were occupied by Antonio Jaconelli's café (with its 'real' Italian ice cream), H.J. Murray's hairdresser shop, and Alexander Watt Gillies' bakery. In 1922, some four years after the bakery had moved across the road, Glasgow businessman Thomas McLean opened a chemist shop in Oakbank. This business was later continued by his son, James, who relocated to premises further along Cumbernauld Road. These premises were extended around 1975, when McLean took over adjoining premises which previously had been a millinery run by the Misses McKinlay. Later occupants of the shops at Oakbank included the Coatbridge Co-operative Society, who had grocery and drapery departments here. For a period, before the advent of 'talkies' in the 1930s, the single-storey extension to the rear of Oakbank was used by local businessman David Kilpatrick for the showing of silent films.

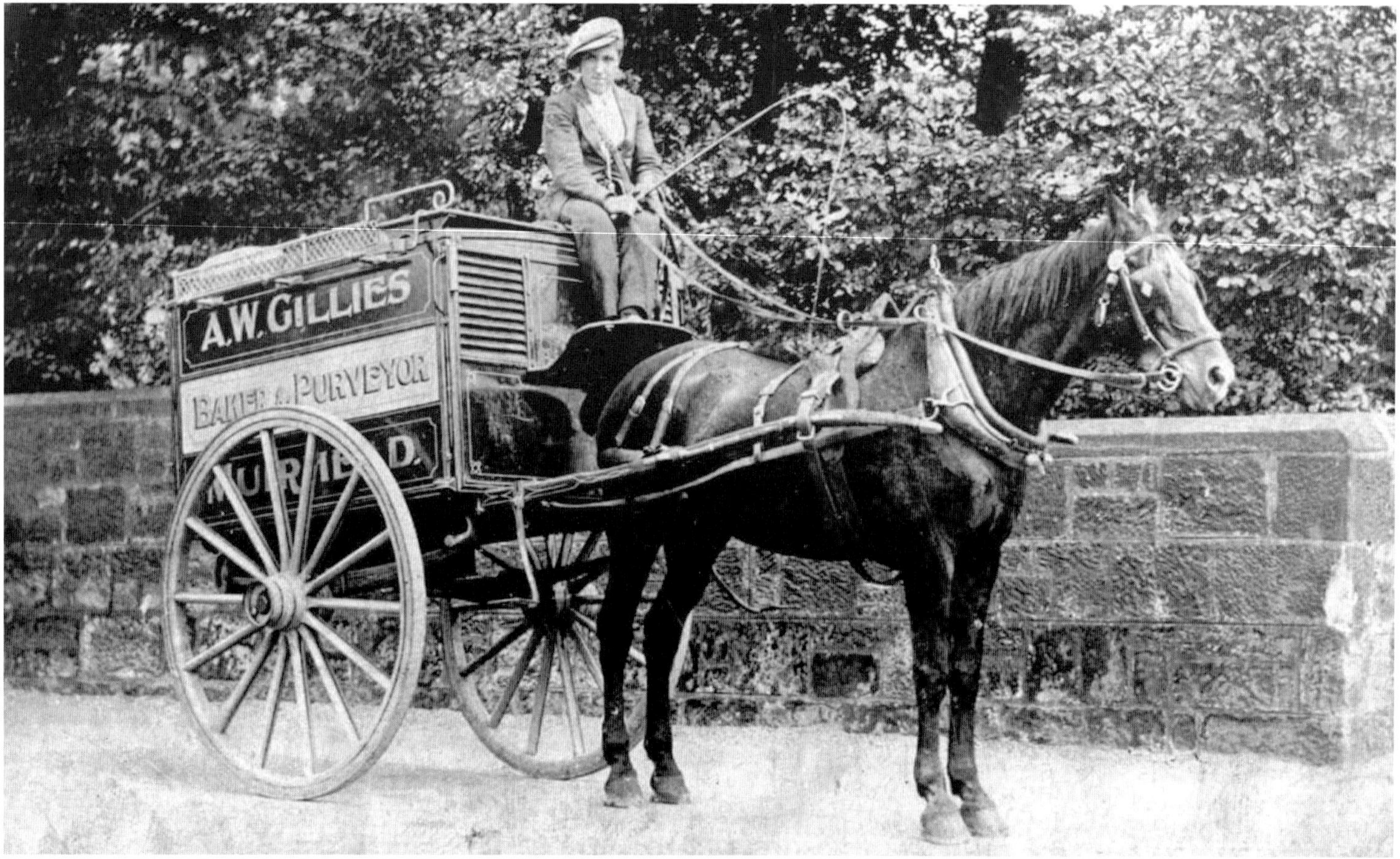

This horse-drawn delivery cart was one of several operated by local baker and purveyor A.W. Gillies. Gillies, who started his business around 1910, was a well-respected baker whose products, especially his 'hot plate goods', won many awards at major exhibitions. Many of the 'purveys' supplied for local social events came from Gillies' Muirhead shop, and his tuppenny bags of cake cuttings were especially popular with the local children. Initially, all the products sold in his Oakbank bakery were prepared in his bakehouse situated in Lindsaybeg Road. However, in 1918, having outgrown the Oakbank shop, he moved across the road into a larger shop with adjacent bakehouse. As the business prospered, he replaced the horse-drawn carts with a fleet of motorised vans, before eventually opening branches in Airdrie, Coatbridge, Gartcosh and Stepps. A member of the Executive Committee of the Scottish Master Bakers' Association, and a prolific exhibitor, Gillies died in 1937 while engaged in a pair's game on the local bowling green. In the 1950s the business was sold and the bakery shops were closed.

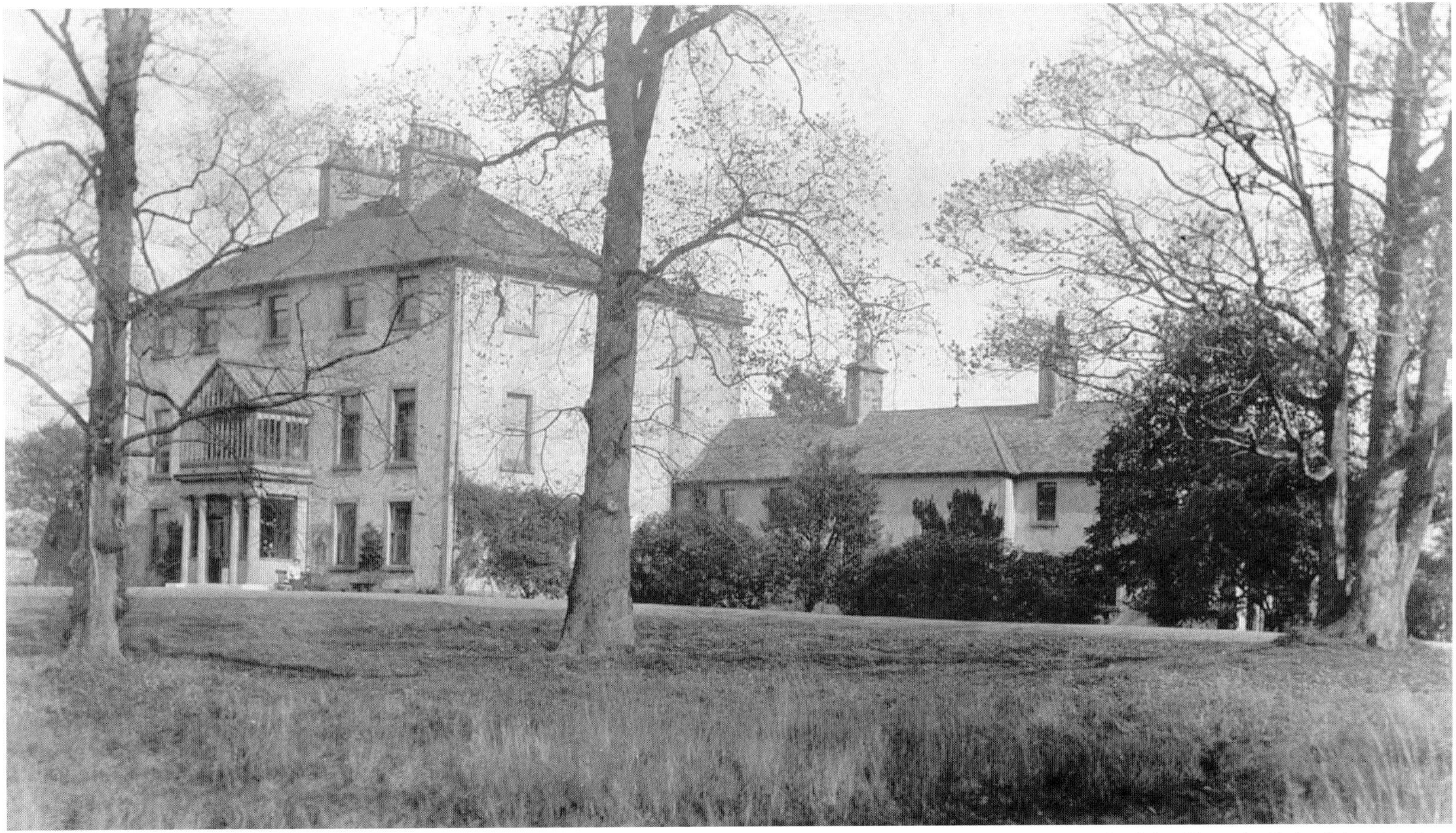

By the mid 1920s, when this photograph of Garnkirk House was taken, the original seventeenth-century mansion (which had been built for John Dunlop, a Glasgow banking merchant) had been demolished and replaced by this new building. Built around 1820, this mansion had been designed by Glasgow architect David Hamilton for Mark Sprot, the then owner of Garnkirk Estate. In 1874 the 1,457-acre estate passed to his grandson, Colonel Sir Alexander Sprot (who later inherited a second estate, Stravithie, near St Andrews in Fife). In the early 1920s, when Garnkirk Estate was being broken up by the colonel, a 5,610 yards-long golf course was laid out within its grounds. This was designed by the legendary Scottish golfer James Braid. Central to the new golf course was Garnkirk House, which was acquired as a clubhouse by the newly formed Crow Wood Golf Club. In 1932 Garnkirk House was sold to the prominent Glasgow insurance broker, Alexander Rennie Stenhouse, who then had it substantially rebuilt. However, in 1955, a few years after Stenhouse's death, Garnkirk House was once again acquired by the golf club and it has remained in their hands ever since.

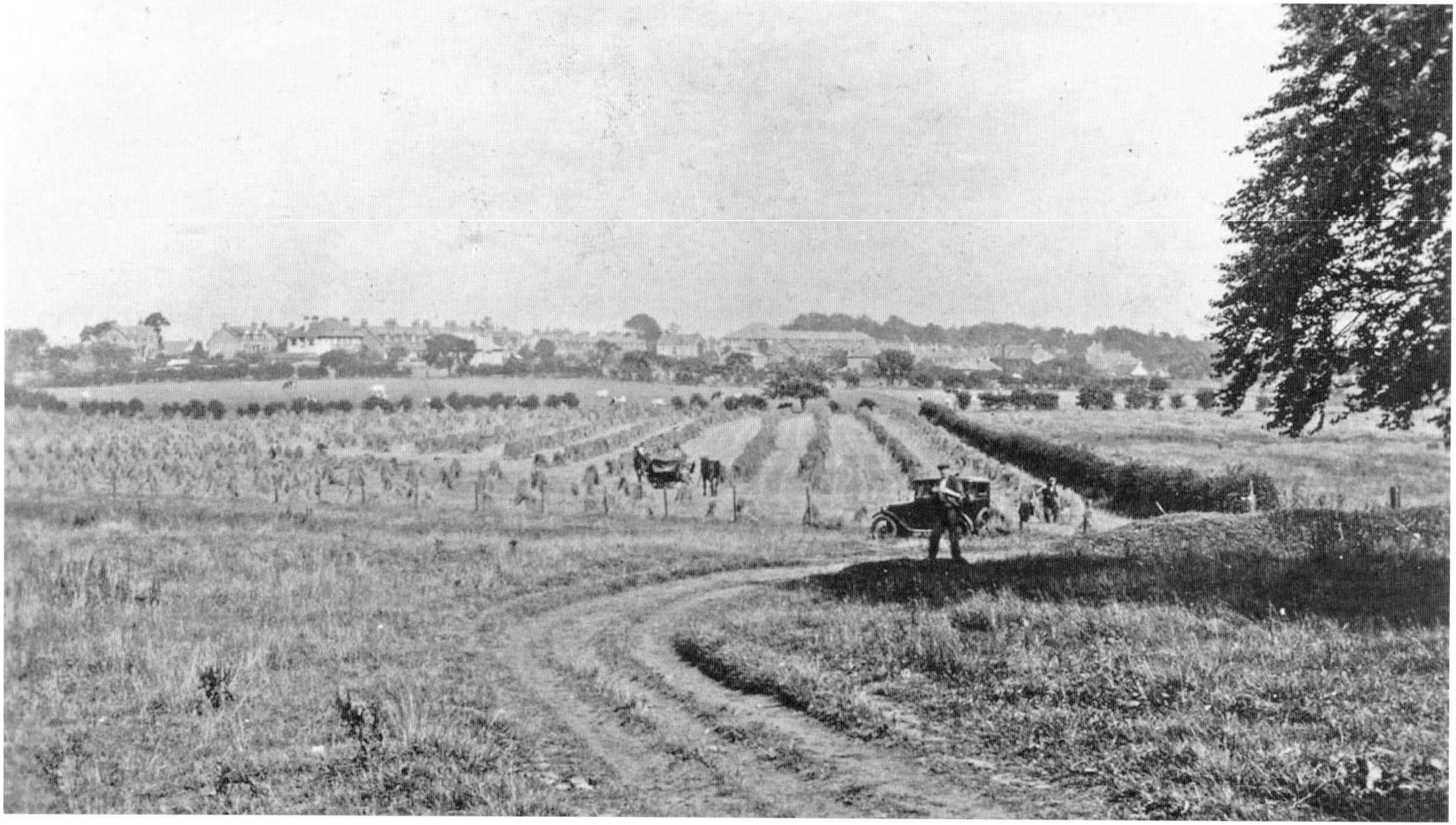

In this 1920s view harvesting is being carried out in one of the fields belonging to Woodhead Farm. This annual event in the farming calendar would most likely have occasioned a visit by the Rev. William Davidson, the Chryston Parish Church minister. The Rev. Davidson made a practice of visiting each and every one of the local farms during harvest thanksgiving and, with the farmer and farm workers, would conduct a short service in the fields to give thanks to God for the harvest. The fields of Woodhead Farm lay on either side of Woodhead Road. It was one of the older farms in the district and was farmed by George Jackson from the 1890s until around 1913. Thereafter, it was briefly farmed by William Bankier, although by 1925, when the farm was put up for sale by Garnkirk Estate, it was in the hands of Hugh Walker. In the sale catalogue at that time it is described as comprising a farmhouse, a modern byre for 24 cattle, a boiler house and eighteen acres of woodland. It was last farmed by Jim Walker, before being sold to its present owner, who now operates a successful bed and breakfast establishment from the farmhouse.

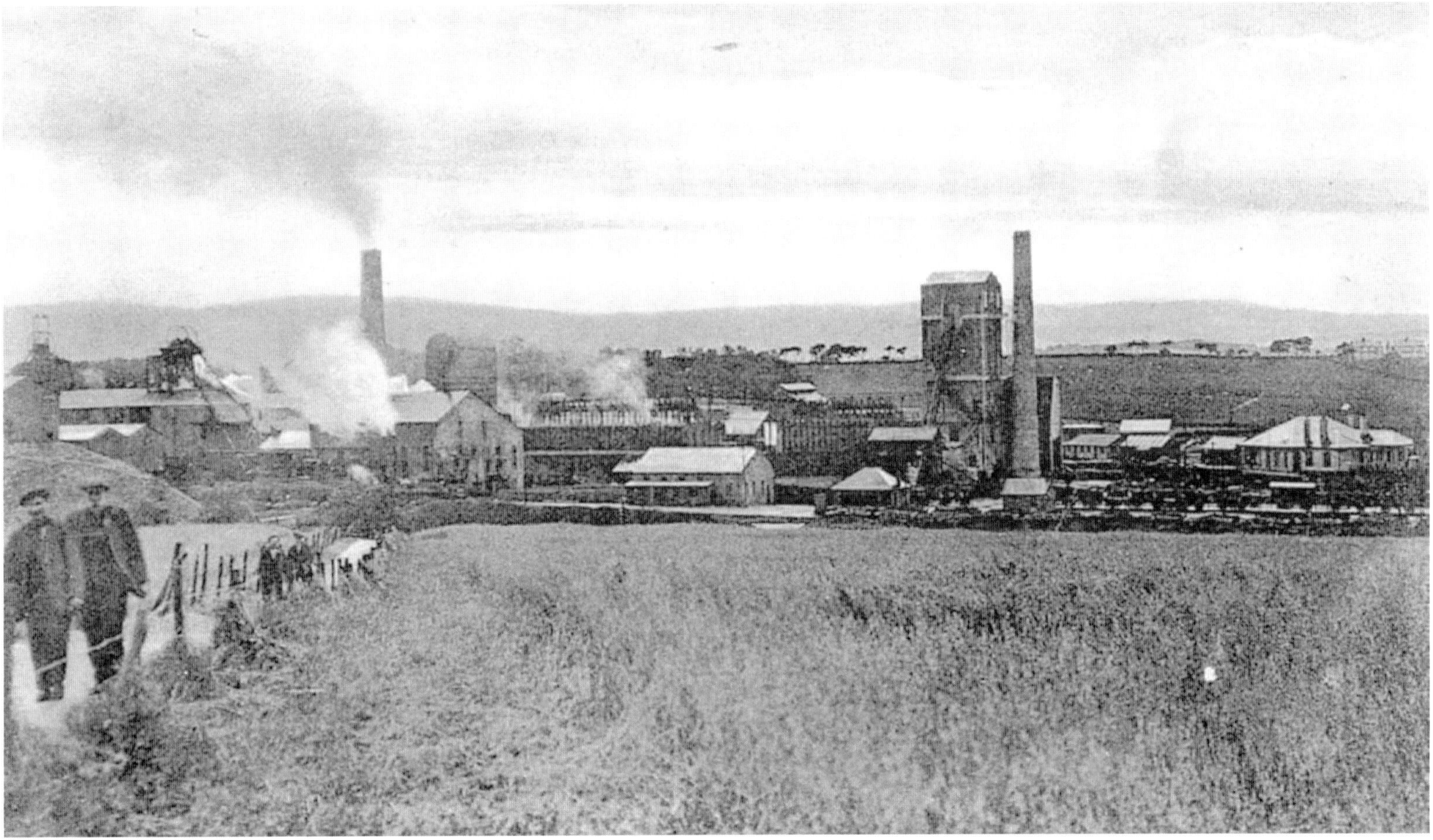

On 18 September 1959 the mining village of Bridgend was devastated by the loss of 47 miners when acrid smoke from a fire overcame some of Auchengeich Colliery's day shift workers just as they were 300 yards short of the pit entrance and safety. This incident – one of the worst mining disasters in Scotland – ultimately led to the closure of the colliery and the dispersal of its workforce to nearby collieries at Bedlay and Cardowan. Auchengeich Colliery had commenced production in 1905 and was one of several owned by coal masters James Nimmo & Company. In addition to coal, various other fuels were extracted from the high quality coke produced in the coking ovens. In this 1920s photograph the coke oven plant can be seen to the right. With the closure of the colliery, the village of Bridgend was abandoned. Today, all traces of the colliery and the village have gone, with the exception of the Miners' Welfare Hall, which was opened in 1923 on Gartferry Road.

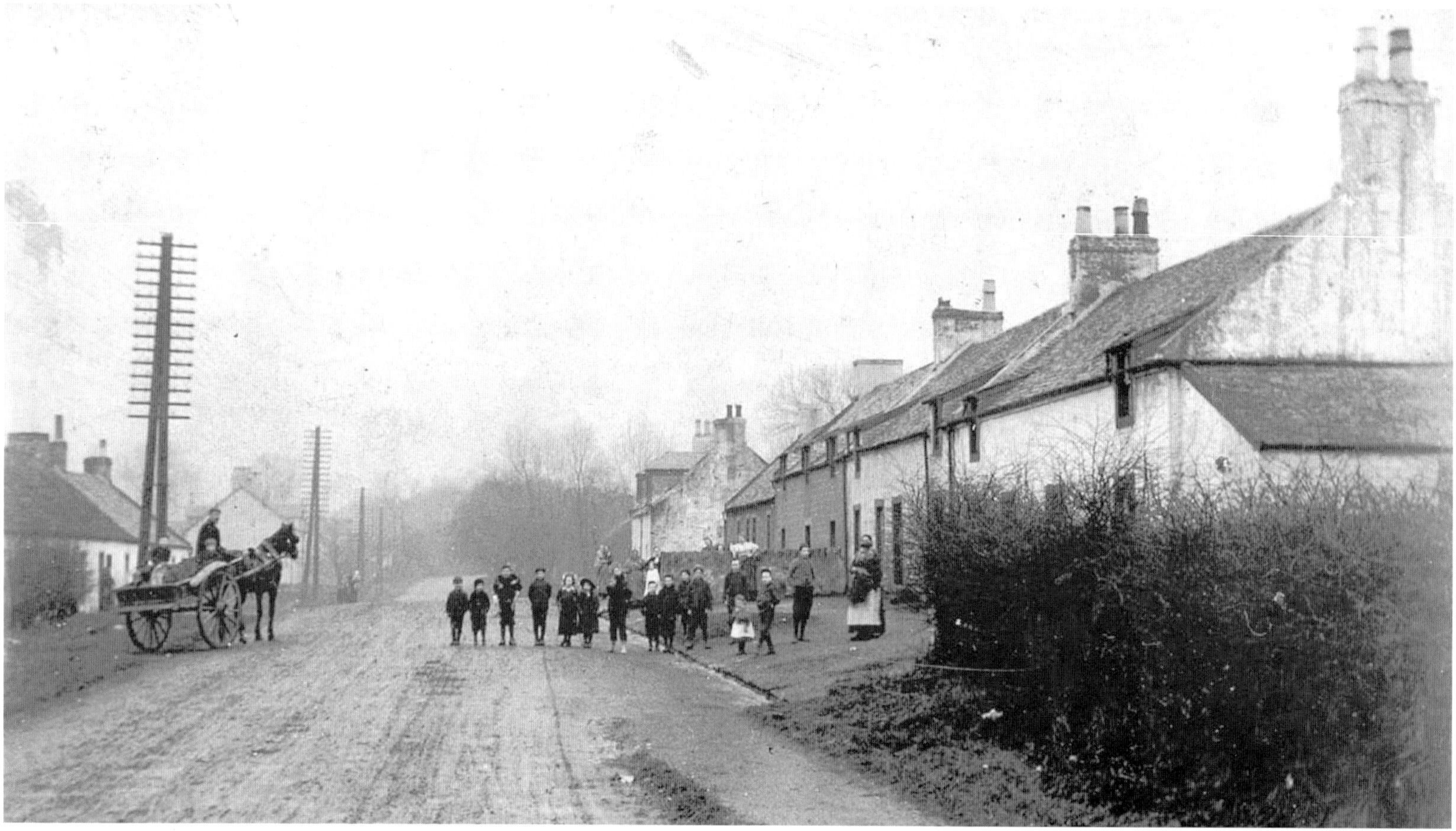

In this view, taken around 1910 and looking west, some of the 35 properties which comprised the original hamlet of Moodiesburn can be seen on Cumbernauld Road, just to the east of Moodiesburn crossroads. The occupants of these properties, some of whom can be seen here, were mostly families of the workers at the local quarry and fireclay works. By 1841 the population of the hamlet had amounted to no more than 220 persons. Although there was substantial building activity from the 1930s onwards, this was all concentrated on greenfield sites to the north of the original hamlet. Today, all that remains of the original hamlet is the row of single-storey cottages alongside the horse and cart and the two-storey building whose whitewashed gable end which can be seen at the crossroads, just beyond the horse. These cottages, known locally as Burnside Cottages, were bought by James Beattie in 1910 from coal masters James Nimmo & Company, and are thought to be about 200 years old. The properties on the opposite side of the road have all gone, primarily as a result of road-widening schemes of the late 1930s and 1950s.

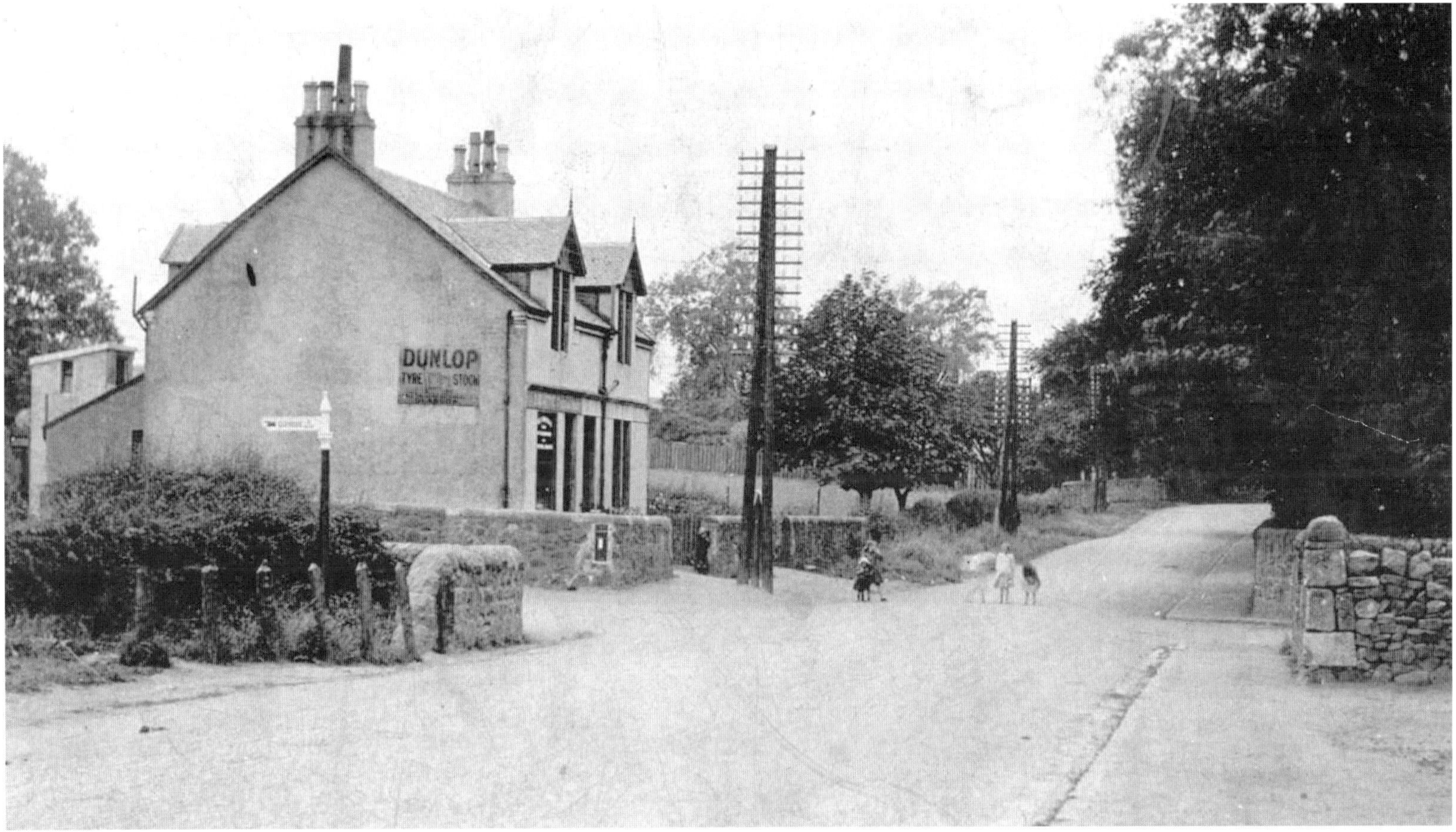

In this photograph, also taken around 1910, the two-storey building at Moodiesburn crossroads seen in the previous photograph is shown more clearly. Known locally as McKay Place, it was built around 1904 for Samuel Beattie. Beattie utilised the ground floor of the property as a general grocery shop and living quarters, and the upper floor as accommodation for his relatives. To the rear of the property were outside steps. These formed a separate access to the upper level, which comprised two flats, leading off from a small central hallway. These flats were later converted into one home. The area around the property once formed part of Beattie's extensive garden, where he grew a wide range of prize-winning blooms, which he then exhibited at the annual Chryston Flower Shows. In later years (until around the 1980s) the grocery shop was run by Jimmy and Lucy Laird, however it has since been converted into a private house. The road leading off to the left is Avenuehead Road, which, in turn, leads to the former mining village of Glenboig. The road to the right is Stoneyetts Road, which led to Gartferry House, Bridgend, and Stoneyetts Hospital.

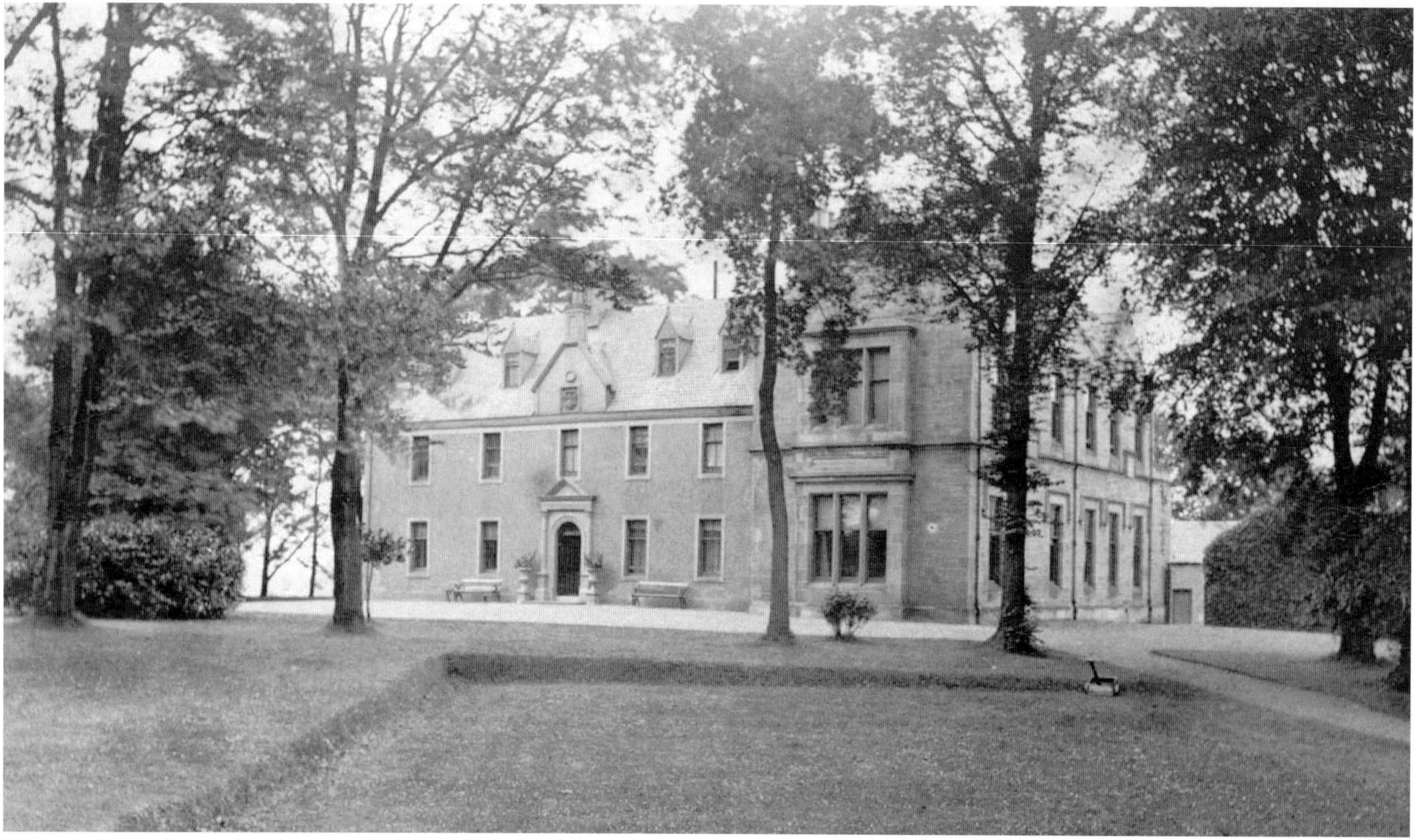

Gartferry House (known locally as the 'Big Hoose') was built in the early seventeenth century for the Robertsons of Bedlay. In addition to the house, the 38-acre estate also included stables and estate workers' cottages. In more recent times, relatively speaking, its best-known occupant was Glasgow textile manufacturer Henry Rawson Taggart. He occupied the house from the 1890s until his death in the early 1920s. During Taggart's tenure, Gartferry House was extended and a supply of electricity was fed into it from nearby Auchengeich Colliery. A generous local benefactor, Taggart, whose estate encompassed the mining village of Bridgend, not only provided financial assistance for the widows of the miners, but also gave them employment on his estate. After Taggart's death, and until 1924, the estate was briefly run by his son before being sold to coal masters James Nimmo & Company, who later demolished the house. In 1976 a library and a community education centre were built on the site of the house.